THE TASK OF
GESTALT PSYCHOLOGY

THE TASK OF

GESTALT

PSYCHOLOGY

BY WOLFGANG KÖHLER

WITH AN INTRODUCTION
BY CARROLL C. PRATT

PRINCETON, NEW JERSEY
PRINCETON UNIVERSITY PRESS

It was fitting that Wolfgang Köhler should have been among the first to be invited to deliver the Herbert S. Langfeld Memorial Lectures. The two, Langfeld and Köhler, were firm friends for a half century. They had taken their degrees together at Berlin, and they shared many interests, professional and social. Their association over the years was warmly sympathetic and one that was frequently renewed.

None of us could have known, that night in mid-November 1966, as we listened to Köhler's final lecture in a series of four that we were hearing the last major disclosure by the last of the great ones of Gestalt psychology. At the close he showed the famous film of the chimpanzees on Tenerife which he had taken more than half a century earlier, and he laughed with his audience at the antics of the apes that had given him his first insight into *Einsicht*. When the lights were turned up, Köhler's listeners rose and gave the remarkable man a long ovation.

He died before his manuscript had been polished into the form only he could have given it. Fortunately for us and for psychological posterity Wolfgang Köhler was blessed with devotees who held to him by intellectual as well as other ties. Shortly after his death three of them banded together to put into publishable form a manuscript prepared for oral presentation to the Princeton audiences. This group—Solomon Asch, Mary Henle, and Edwin Newman—has the everlasting gratitude of all of us connected with the Langfeld Lectures. To preserve Köhler's characteristically direct style while rounding out his phrases to meet the demands of the printed page required a special wisdom.

The Committee charged with responsibility for the Series—J. L. Kennedy, J. M. Notterman, C. C. Pratt, and the undersigned—was also fortunate in having to look no further than to its own membership to find a sensitive appreciator of Wolfgang Köhler. The introduction by Pratt adds a theme to the history of psychology that could not have originated in any other source. Pratt's confreres on the Committee record here their appreciation of him.

For the Herbert S. Langfeld
Memorial Lectures Committee
Frank A. Geldard, Chairman

CONTENTS

WOLFGANG KÖHLER • 1887-1967

WOLFGANG KÖHLER • 1887-1967

The first sentence in the preface to Köhler's *The Place of Value in a World of Facts* proclaims boldly that the purpose of the book is philosophical. It is dedicated to Ralph Barton Perry, and ranges widely over areas which at the time most American psychologists would have feared to tread, perhaps because during their student days they had become infected by Titchener's pontifical proclamation that science has nothing to do with values or by the behaviorists' thumping insistence on facts, facts, facts, nothing but facts. Some twenty years earlier Köhler had published *Die physischen Gestalten in Ruhe und im stationären Zustand* (1920), dedicated to Carl Stumpf, a brilliant work full of new facts which he and the other members of the triumvirate, Wertheimer and Koffka, and their students were bringing to light, all set in relation to a rigid framework of physical field theory. *Gestaltpsychologie* was already on the way to becoming *Gestalttheorie*, for Köhler insisted throughout his life that the phenomenal world is for science the only world open to inspection and that the initial data of this world are Gestalten no matter from what angle or branch of science they may be reported.

It must have been a source of satisfaction in his later years for Köhler to note how pervasive this view had become, not only in science, but also in practical affairs: doctors, economists, ecologists, conservationists, and even those who bulldoze our landscape— some of them, at any rate—seem increasingly aware that an operation in one place is often a contradiction in terms, for any one place may be part of a larger area in which the operation will produce unexpected and sometimes disastrous results.

These two books, along with everything else Köhler did and said and wrote, furnish striking evidence of an active and original mind that for well over half a century grappled with all sorts of questions beyond the usual range and concern of the experimental psychologist in academe. Köhler was a philosopher, psychologist, physiologist, physicist, humanist, a great lover of nature, travel and art, especially music, and a man whose concern with public affairs made it possible, even if not pleasant, for him to descend from the ivory tower whenever and wherever he felt he could be of assistance.

Die physischen Gestalten and the earlier book that soon became so popular, *The Mentality of Apes* (first German edition, *Intelligenzprüfungen an Anthropoiden*, 1917) undoubtedly had a good deal to do in securing for Köhler his appointment in 1921 as Director of the Institute of Psychology in the University of Berlin. There Köhler reigned supreme until he decided to leave Germany for good in 1935. His manner with colleagues and students in those days often seemed aloof and at times disconcerting. Yet students who worked closely with him were deeply devoted disciples, and many others who saw a good deal of him were convinced that his austerity of manner (he was born of German parents in Estonia, but came back with them to Germany when he was a young boy) concealed a shyness that bothered him in all his human relations. In later years in this country the underlying shyness remained, but the surface more frequently revealed a gentle nature of great charm.

With the death of Wundt in 1920 the rivalry between Berlin and Leipzig came to an end. Berlin now replaced Leipzig by a wide margin as the undisputed Mecca for students in Europe, America, and the Orient who wanted to find out what was going on in psychology in postwar Germany. Köhler's Institute was in one end of the former Emperor's palace, and there he and his colleagues and students published in their own journal, *Psychologische Forschung*, an astonishing number of studies, largely in the field of perception, that in a short period of time made it necessary for professors and graduate students in psychology and related subjects the world over to learn how to talk knowingly, if not always sympathetically, about Gestalt psychology.

Köhler at his best was such a brilliant lecturer that students flocked to his general course in great numbers. The lectures were carefully prepared, and students were often held spellbound by the fortunate combination in one man of so many attractive gifts: handsome appearance and an impressive bearing, a fine sonorous speaking voice, a smooth flow of words guided by a sensitive ear for sound and *le mot juste*, a good sense of timing and cadence, and the art of developing a theme as though it were a fugue moving relentlessly to an inexorable conclusion through a wealth of philosophy and art as well as science.

In the fall of 1934 after Köhler had delivered at Harvard the William James lectures which formed the bulk of *The Place of Value*, he knew he could no longer delay making a painful decision. Should he return to Hitler's Germany?

Before and after Hitler came to power Köhler had repeatedly warned his countrymen and especially his colleagues in the University about the dangers of Nazism. He used every available means to spread the alarm—

in one instance a long attack on the regime in a Berlin newspaper which aroused so much interest that extra copies were rushed from the press to the streets. Once after storm troopers had prowled around his Institute and interfered with his seminar, he complained bitterly to the Rector Magnificus and later, according to one report, gave the Minister of Education such a tongue-lashing that the official was taken aback and in awed tones expressed to Köhler his astonishment that a mere professor would dare to speak to him in such fashion. "But," he said, recovering his self-assurance, "there's nothing I care to do for you. Heil Hitler."

Friends of Köhler admired his courage, though at the same time they were apprehensive lest in some mysterious way he might one day be removed from the scene. But nothing happened. And also nothing of importance happened within the University where Köhler had hoped he might arouse his colleagues to take some sort of action. In this effort he met only frustration. Most of the professors either dismissed the Nazis as a bunch of thugs who could never gain control of the political machinery of the most advanced society in the world or refused as scholars to become involved in matters that were none of their business or outside their proper spheres of influence.

So in 1934 Köhler reached a critical turning point in his career. By that time the Nazis were in command pretty much from top to bottom, and it seemed highly improbable that anything could be done to dislodge them. In an atmosphere so hostile and destructive to everything he stood for he knew it would be impossible to carry on his work. In both sorrow and anger he finally decided to resign from the Institute and forsake his homeland. He returned for a short time to Berlin to wind up matters there, and then in the fall of 1935 accepted from Mr. Aydelotte an invitation to become a research professor at Swarthmore College, where with hardly any interruption at all he was able in that friendly community to resume the kind of research and writing that were so necessary to his peace of mind. During the summer of 1937 he and Mrs. Köhler and their daughter Karen were on Monhegan, an island off the coast of Maine. There with the help of Robert MacLeod he put the finishing touches to *The Place of Value*. A few years later the Köhlers bought a place near Dartmouth in the hills of New Hampshire, where after his retirement they spent the better part of each year.

Wertheimer and Koffka were now also established in this country and the triumvirate preached the gospel of Gestalt psychology with unremitting zeal, for they found their American colleagues far gone in the sins of introspectionism and behaviorism. But there was reason for hope, or so at least thought Köhler, because the sins were not so much those of commission as of omission. The data of introspection and behavior are both part of the phenomenal world and thus suitable materials for scientific study, but in singling out sensations and reflexes by an overrefined and artificial analysis and then concentrating almost exclusively on them the students in both disciplines had overlooked or left out the most important items—the full-blown forms, the Gestalten—of behavior and consciousness that are the very essence of mental life and cannot be equated to the sum of so and so many sensations and reflexes. This theme runs through a good part of Köhler's *Gestalt Psychology* (1929), a book that served as a kind of advance notice, as it were, to American psychologists of the nature of the campaign the triumvirate would wage in their new home.

One phrase frequently associated with the unique properties of organized wholes was actually not used by the Gestalt psychologists, but nevertheless gave them no end of trouble: *The whole is more than the sum of its parts.* Many American psychologists were inclined to regard that statement as the major theme of Gestalt psychology and proceeded to attack it as the quintessence of absurdity.

Köhler often said that he wished his critics would remember that what he really said was that the whole is *different* from the sum of the parts.

When the tones c and g are sounded together they produce a quality which in music is called the Fifth. That quality is neither in the c nor the g, nor does it depend on those particular notes. Any two tones with the ratio 2/3 will be recognized immediately as a Fifth no matter in what region of the scale they may be played. Fifthness is a Gestalt which is different from either or any of its parts, and no amount of knowledge about the parts in isolation would ever give the remotest hint as to what Fifthness is like. *Solvitur audiendo.*

One topic in the 1929 book, if it had been treated more explicitly and clearly, might have explained an attitude on the part of the triumvirate that often puzzled those who observed the eager intensity with which the three men entered into almost every dispute going on among American psychologists. They seemed to love to do battle, and there were enough disagreements on the American academic scene to keep them well occupied—especially Köhler, who was in constant demand as a lecturer all over the country and was by far the most vocal of the three men—in revealing to both sides of a dispute the way in which the errors of their respective positions could be corrected by the insights of Gestalt psychology.

The bitterest dispute in the twenties and early thirties was between the classical psychologists (the followers of Wundt and Titchener) and the behaviorists. The younger psychologists of today can hardly imagine the violence of that dispute or the vitriolic manner in which it was carried on. Members of one side often looked upon their opponents as no better than high-grade morons in their addle-brained foozles about the subject matter of psychology. Köhler stood above that battle. He attacked both sides for their sins, especially their treatment of sensation and reflex in atomistic fashion, but never entered into the wrangle that was going on *between* the two sides. Why was that? The answer was implied in his *Gestalt Psychology* (esp. Chap. III), but as it often went unnoticed Köhler made his position much clearer in later seminars and lectures.

Part of the answer was clear enough in Köhler's insistence that behavioral and introspective data are both phenomenal events and that any difference between them is either an insoluble metaphysical riddle—the body-mind problem—or more likely just tweedledum and tweedledee. But there was a more cogent reason for his remaining aloof.

Phenomenal data in any science are points of departure, the first steps in the building of a conceptual framework into which the data will fit. In and of themselves they have no special interest or significance. They derive their importance from the degree to which they serve to test an hypothesis, validate a theory, assist in further speculation, lend support to a mathematical model, or what not. Hypotheses and theories are logical constructs, not observations, although observations are necessary for their formulation. The world of modern physics is many degrees removed from the phenomenal world where it started and to which it must always be able to return. The phenomenal world is the one in which we all live: houses, tables, chairs, automobiles, rocks, mountains, rivers, and lakes, etc.; but the world of physics is very different; it has been steadily moving further out of sight ever since the days of Galileo and Newton, until before long it will consist of little more than mathematical formulae.

So it is in psychology. The phenomenal world is the same as that to which the physicist must always return for verification of his formulae, but for the psychologist this world is the starting point for the construction of hypotheses about what goes on inside the living organism. The way people think, feel, behave, perceive, remember, solve problems, etc. is clearly the result in part of neural processes, most of which unfortunately at present can only be guessed at, but which it is the business of psychology to approach by observing the phenomenal data of introspection and behavior. These data may be reports on the apparent size of objects, the mistakes in recalling a list of nonsense syllables, the number of errors a rat makes in learning a maze, and innumerable other events revealed by living organisms. Since the events themselves are important only for the part they play in the constructing of physiological hypotheses, any wrangling over what events are suitable subject matter for psychology and what are not is completely irrelevant. Anything is all right that helps build an hypothesis.

The situation is somewhat analogous to the relation between a patient's account of his symptoms and the doctor's diagnosis. The doctor is not interested in aches, pains, short breath, nausea, and other varieties of malaise as such. These symptoms are merely clues that help him in his diagnosis as to what is wrong with the patient's internal workings. Since the initial data of psychology, and of all science for that matter, are to be regarded as clues, it makes no difference whether they are objective or subjective or mental or physical or public or private, whatever those words may mean. So the big battle of the twenties and thirties in American psychology aroused little interest in Köhler.

This view that the data of one science should be translated or converted into the language of an older and more highly developed discipline is a form of reductionism that a good many American psychologists strongly oppose. They argue that psychology has a huge area still to explore and that no time should be lost in futile speculation about physiological hypotheses. They belong to the Nothing But Society, whereas Köhler preferred to join the Something More Society. The members of the Something More Society believe that psychological phenomena have been raked over enough and that no real advance can now be made until psychologists begin to look around for something more.

The way in which Köhler's mind worked in the field of physiological hypotheses is nicely illustrated in his famous paper on the time-error (*Psychologische Forschung*, 1923). Fechner had duly noted and named the time-error more than sixty years earlier, but nothing much had been done since that time except to regard the thing as an error and try to get rid of it either by reversing the order of presentation of the stimuli or reducing the preponderance of judgments in the direction of increase (the negative time-error) by leaving out one or two of the stimuli at the top end of the comparison series. Köhler chose to regard the phenomenon not as an error, but rather as a possible clue to some physiological mechanism.

Borak had suggested a year or two earlier that the negative time-error may be due to the enhancement of the impression of the second stimulus by the physiological after-effect left over from the first stimulus. Köhler was led to propose as an alternative that the after-effect of the first stimulus remained as an independent *sinking* trace in relation to which the second stimulus was accordingly judged too frequently in the direction of increase. Köhler was delighted to note that these two hypotheses would lead to diametrically opposite results if the time-interval between standard and comparison stimuli were lengthened from the usual 4 seconds to 8, 12, 16, 20 seconds, etc. The enhancement of the second impression in Borak's hypothesis would become less with longer time-intervals, and the magnitude of the negative time-error should therefore steadily decrease, whereas according to Köhler's hypothesis the time-error should increase.

The elaborate experiments reported in Köhler's long paper were by no means merely another variation in dealing with a well-known phenomenon. They were expressly designed as a crucial test of two physiological hypotheses. The results were unequivocal. In all the series of judgments with several different kinds of stimuli the magnitude of the negative time-error always increased with every lengthening of the time-interval between standard and comparison stimuli. Köhler's hypothesis thus seemed the more plausible assumption to make regarding the physiological mechanism or mnemonic trace involved. Köhler's curve plotting the course of the *sinking trace* soon found its way into the literature of mnemonics as well as psychophysics, where it still often appears in spite of Köhler's ready acceptance of Lauenstein's argument a decade later that the curve should be replaced by a different set of curves and given an entirely different interpretation.

Otto von Lauenstein was one of Köhler's favorite students in the Institute at Berlin. In 1937 he went to England, but planned to leave for this country in 1939 to take up a position at Rutgers University. He returned to Germany during the summer, and when war broke out in September he sent a cable to Rutgers saying that he was not able to cross the border. He was seriously wounded while serving in the army, was sent back to the front in the last days of the war, and since that time no one has heard anything about him.

In 1932 Lauenstein had published an article in the *Psychologische Forschung* in which he gave it as his opinion that Köhler's concept of the sinking trace was bad Gestalt psychology. The trace just can't sink in a vacuum, as it were. That would be elementarism of the worst kind. The trace must sink because something is pulling it down to a lower level. And if it can be pulled down it ought to be possible to pull it up (a positive time-error) by the interpolation of a stimulus-background appreciably above the stimuli being judged. That is exactly what Lauenstein did, and he was able to show conclusively that the time-error can be made positive or negative depending on the levels of the interpolated background stimuli. He therefore introduced the concept of physiological assimilation as the mechanism that would best account for any kind of time-error. At about the same time and for several years thereafter a rash of experiments broke out in this country pointing in much the same direction. These and many similar studies were treated in great detail some years later in the first sections of Helson's impressive *Adaptation-level Theory* (1964).

Köhler was pleased with Lauenstein's work, especially with the way he had shown that from the point of view of Gestalt psychology the Herr Professor himself had goofed in his interpretation of the time-error. In this country he occasionally referred with a wry grin to Lauenstein's study as an indication that at least in his Institute the German student was not an intellectual slave to the ideas of the master. Had not one of his own students shown that the *Gestalttheoretiker* himself had made an egregious blunder in the application of his own point of view?

A number of critics attacked Köhler for his work on the time-error, as well as many other topics, not on the basis of the facts turned up, but rather because it seemed to them so wholly unnecessary to mess about in brain physiology, or brain mythology, as they often scornfully called it. In the case of the time-error one of the experimental variables was the time-interval between the presentation of the standard and comparison stimuli. Why was it, they asked, that for over half a century no psychophysicist had ever been bright enough to find out what the effect would be of lengthening that interval? To the members of the Nothing But Society it seemed patently obvious that no reference or appeal to physiology was needed to take that step or to plan for new procedures or observations in any area of psychology. They argued that the construction of physiological concepts was likely to be no more than the spinning of circular arguments, in that properties assigned to the nervous system were derived from the very observations the concepts were supposed to explain. Unperturbed by his critics, Köhler effectively answered them in his *Dynamics in Psychology* (1940, esp. pp. 115-126) and in a number of later articles, and then went serenely ahead with his speculations about the brain; in the last years of his life he was patiently seeking more evidence in support of isomorphism, the doctrine which had been foreshadowed in Wertheimer's paper on the phi-phenomenon in 1912 and elaborated in detail in Köhler's *Die physische Gestalten.*

It is matter for regret that none of the members of the Gestalt triumvirate wrote a detailed treatise on the philosophy and psychology of art. An article by Koffka was published in the Bryn Mawr *Symposium on Art* (1940), but many important questions had to be left only partially answered. Any of the three men could have done an imposing volume on the subject, for all of them loved art and knew a great deal about it, as their conversation, lectures, and writings revealed on innumerable occasions; they had developed concepts in Gestalt psychology which, with a little shift of emphasis and illustration, were directly applicable to some of the central problems in aesthetic theory.

Köhler's great love was music, although any form of art was more than likely to capture his interest. Music was a great source of comfort as well as pleasure to him. He was a man of moods. His courtly manner and amiable disposition at times seemed clouded over. Music more than almost anything else was capable of restoring the smile and cheerful expression. He was a good pianist, a lover of the great German classics, among whom, however, he did not count Wagner.

The writings of Köhler and also Koffka contain so many references to the nature of art that it has not been difficult for a number of philosophers and a few psychologists to give a new direction to aesthetic theory on the basis of Gestalt psychology. This trend is not very well known among students of general experimental psychology, but it should be taken into account in any effort to understand the wide influence that Köhler's writings have had. His ideas were making their way at a time when the rapid and astonishing growth of interest in art of all kinds in this country brought with it a new and lively concern for aesthetics, art history, musicology, criticism, and other scholarly by-products of that interest.

One of the marked contrasts between Gestalt psychology and classical psychology may be seen in the treatment of perception. For Titchener, perception was handled as an assemblage of sensations and as something that always has a meaning derived from past experience. The perception of distance, for example, must obviously be the result of learning. The retina is bidimensional, and there can thus be no stimulus for distance nor any sensation of distance. Yet we seem quite immediately and directly to *see* distance, said Titchener (*A Beginner's Psychology*, 1918, p. 117). How does that come about? What happens is that a context of kinaesthetic and visual sensations and images accrues to the bidimensional core and confers on it the *meaning* of distance. The unaided eye cannot *perceive* distance, however palpable distance may seem. Distance is a learned illusion.

In the study of perception Gestalt psychology assigned a minor role to sensations and meaning, sensations because they are more or less artificial abstractions that rarely appear in unfettered observations, and meaning because it is too much like a wastebasket into which anything that does not fit neatly into the rubrics of sensation and image can be dropped and dismissed. Gestalt psychology in many ways represents a critical reformulation of nativism, a view that would insist that in explaining psychological phenomena no appeal should be made to past experience until every other possibility has been exhausted.

The important and salient characteristics of perception are tridimensionality, curvatures, movement, slants, groupings, shapes of all kinds, contours, the various constancies, chords, melodies, speech, rhythm, diminuendos and crescendos, etc. Such phenomena are Gestalten, not sensations, and they have their own laws and methods of investigation that have little resemblance to the principles and procedures of classical psychology.

In addition to these characteristics of perception there stands forth in many instances yet another quality more prominent than anything else, an overall feature that may be retained long after other aspects have faded from memory, if indeed they were ever noticed at all. The friendliness of a face is more likely to be remembered than the width of the nose, the distance between the eyes, the part in the hair, the shape of the lips, the size of the ears, or even the color of the eyes. Friendliness of expression is a *tertiary quality* along with countless others in perception that are best described by words that are also used for moods. A room appears drab and inhospitable, the waves of the sea are agitated, the voice over the radio pinched and monotonous, the face of our neighbor's child sprightly and gay, the gesture of the speaker imperative, etc. The development of the nature and conditions of tertiary qualities has been one of the more important contributions of Gestalt psychology to aesthetics.

Tertiary qualities make their appearance in art more often and more strikingly than anywhere else and are regarded by many authorities as the very essence of the appeal and tenacious hold that art has had in all times and places. The music of Beethoven is often powerful and even titanic, although as in the case of Michelangelo's sculpture there are many examples of gentle tenderness; the faces of Renaissance madonnas are wistful and sad; the music of Mozart frequently is melancholy in spite of the gaiety of its surface; the glass of Chartres glistens with radiant color; many passages in Reger fairly burst with romantic fervor, etc.

Where do these qualities come from? In classical psychology, if they were mentioned at all, they were as likely as not dismissed as a special case of meaning, an association by inference mistakenly assigned in everyday speech to external visual and auditory impressions. But external objects cannot *present* moods and emotions. Emotions and moods are inside the person who has them, not outside.

The views of Lipps and Santayana came to be well known around the turn of the century as somewhat similar answers to the vexed question of aesthetic affectivity. Their clear and straightforward arguments came as a godsend to the classical psychologists and also to the philosophers of that period who were at all concerned with the ancient problem of emotion in art. Lipps' doctrine of empathy was more widely known, partly because it had been elaborated in considerable detail for use in general psychology, especially in the interpretation of geometric-optic illusions, before the author carried it over into aesthetic theory. A landscape may seem tranquil, a mountain majestic, a melody sad because within the observer an incipient mood or emotion is aroused and then erroneously projected into the visual or auditory modalities. The melody itself cannot of course be sad, but the listener calls it that because he is unaware that his own viscera have discharged a tiny bit of sadness. He feels his way into what he hears. The German word *Einfühlung* expresses better the intent of Lipps' idea. The doctrine seemed like a perfect solution of the mystery as to how subjective states, feeling and emotion, find their way into works of art, and it made excellent psychological sense out of the ponderous old assertion that art is the objectification of the subjective. The doctrine was not seriously challenged until Köhler and Koffka criticized it some forty years after Lipps had given it birth.

Santayana's famous statement that beauty is pleasure regarded as the quality of an object embodied a principle very similar to that of empathy. The first term of art is the sensory material, the form. The second term includes the moods and feelings and associations aroused by the first term. In aesthetic experience the second term must fuse with the first in such a way that it appears as an integral part of the object of art. The pleasure is in the object, not in the person—or so it seems. The fusion of first and second terms gives the surface of art a *Scheingefühl*, just as Titchener's theory of meaning had it that the core and context unite to create the illusion of distance.

The attack on empathy when made in full force by Köhler was aimed in various directions. Köhler's chief objection was that empathy solves no problem at all; it merely pushes it back for solution elsewhere. If visual and auditory impressions have no tertiary qualities in their own right, how does it happen that the kinaesthetic, visceral, and organic modalities possess them in such exclusive abundance? Köhler's simple but far-reaching answer consisted of a restatement of the basic tenet of Gestalt psychology. Phenomenal experience, no matter where it comes from, is made up first and foremost of Gestalten, and the tertiary qualities of Gestalten exist no less in visual and auditory impressions than in those from within the body. There is no borrowing or lending back and forth. That would be impossible. An auditory rhythm is auditory, and that's that; but the same rhythm—a Gestalt—may also be visual or tactual, and the graceful lilt, let us say of a waltz rhythm—a tertiary quality—will be present in all three modalities. Gestalten and their tertiary qualities reveal innumerable iconic relations and resemblances across modalities. Therein lies the great power of art, for the moods and feelings of mankind are capable of iconic *presentation* in visual and auditory patterns—a mode obviously far more direct and effective than symbolic *representation*—and when done by the great geniuses of art they become the world's treasures of painting, music, sculpture, ballet, and architecture.

Empathy has little factual evidence to support it, whereas evidence against it was implied in Wertheimer's early paper on the phi-phenomenon. Apparent movement is not the fusion of ocular kinaesthesis and visual quality. The phi-phenomenon takes place quicker than the eye can move and can be made to move in several directions at once, which the eye certainly cannot do. The phi-phenomenon is *sui generis*, pure unadulterated visual quality. When the eye does move, as in reading, it makes quick starts and stops, no matter what the content of the visual field may be. The difference between, let us say, a graceful and awkward line can thus hardly be ascribed to empathic projections of eye movements. By the same reasoning, says Köhler, his enjoyment of the graceful movements of ballet, especially those of Pavlova, is difficult to account for by similar incipient movements in himself, for it would be ludicrously impossible for him to make any such movements. The outbursts of joy in Beethoven's Choral Symphony or the religious fervor in Bach's B-minor Mass are far beyond the humdrum experience of most mortals. Yet untold thousands have been lifted out of themselves by such masterpieces.

A recognition of the power of tertiary qualities restores to the artist his position of pre-eminence among the gods of mankind, a position not accorded him by the doctrines of Lipps and Santayana. Empathy implies that what the lover of art discovers in his objects of admiration are qualities which in the last analysis are projections of his own inner self, not *presentations* which the artist himself has created.

If interest in aesthetic theory continues to gain strength, it is more than likely that Gestalt psychology will exert ever greater influence in that direction. The views of Köhler and Koffka seem designed to give a new lease of life to a body of inquiry that has fascinated scholars for centuries, but which until recent years had revealed little imagination or original thinking. Lipps and Santayana stirred the minds of scholars with what seemed like masterstrokes for the solution of old problems. Gestalt psychology presented a challenge and a new proposal. If the greatness of a work of art is contained within its own formal structure, as the doctrine of tertiary qualities proclaims to be the case, it is the task of global psychophysics to find out what the stimulus conditions are that produce those qualities, and what it is the artist does with his tones and colors to give them the sound of gaiety or the look of serenity. Students of aesthetics will have plenty to do and think about for a long time to come.

Köhler's influence in the more general area of psychology is difficult, if not impossible, to assess at the present time. In a lecture in Europe in 1949 Langfeld said that the main observations, questions, and principles of Gestalt psychology had become part of the mental equipment of every American psychologist, and as early as 1929 Boring wrote that there is little work of broad scope that has not been affected by Gestalt psychology and almost no problem in experimental psychology that had not been brought within the range of that point of view. Köhler himself was not so sanguine. In his address as President of the American Psychological Association in 1959 he pointed to a number of current trends that were struggling along without the benefit of Gestalt psychology, but he ended on an optimistic note. It was time to get rid of schools of psychology, and he felt that the outlook for collaboration among men of differing convictions was steadily improving—a point of view that he himself had done a good deal to promote when he first came to this country.

A few of the many honors that came to Köhler include several degrees from universities in this country and Europe—truly *honoris causa*. Not long before he died on June 11, 1967, at his home in New Hampshire, he had been in Sweden to receive an honorary degree from the University of Uppsala. On the occasion of his 75th birthday, January 21, 1962, a number of friends gathered together in Cambridge at the home of Edwin B. Newman to present him with a *Festschrift* to which a score of admirers from four or five different countries had contributed articles. In 1958 he joined a long list of illustrious scholars whom the University of Edinburgh had invited over the years to deliver the Gifford lectures, and a few years later in Germany he was made an *Ehrenbürger* of Berlin, an honor which had been conferred on only two other Americans: Paul Hindemith and President Kennedy.

Carroll C. Pratt

Pennington, N.J.

THE TASK OF
GESTALT PSYCHOLOGY

I · EARLY
DEVELOPMENTS IN
GESTALT PSYCHOLOGY

I have been invited to talk about Gestalt psychology. This name is often supposed to refer not to a part of general psychology but rather to a particular school or, perhaps, a sect within this science. You will soon see why, and also why this interpretation of the name is entirely misleading.

Not all members of this audience are specialists in psychology. I will, therefore, begin not with a discussion of very special technical issues but with very simple psychological questions and observations.

When, about a hundred years ago, psychology began to develop as a new science, perception was naturally its most readily available subject matter. Those whom we now call Gestalt psychologists did their early work in this field. I will therefore now report on what happened in their investigation of perception. Almost immediately their studies developed in a direction of which most other psychologists of the time did not approve. Why? The way in which the Gestalt psychologists proceeded seemed to the others to be incompatible with a basic principle of science. A young science, it was generally believed, must first consider the most simple facts in its field. Once these are known, the scientist may gradually turn to more complicated situations and try to discover how they can be understood as combinations of the simple elements already known. When applied to the perceptual material studied by the early Gestalt psychologists, the rule was formulated specifically in the following manner. When investigating perception, one has first of all to examine the simplest local facts of which a perceptual field, say the visual field, consists, and to ignore or to remove from these elements all secondary ingredients and disturbances which tend to obscure the true simple nature of the elements.

The early Gestalt psychologists ignored this rule. They proceeded in a different fashion, because they were not interested in those "simple elements," the so-called local sensations. First, they said, we have to inspect perceptual scenes quite impartially, to try to find in these scenes such facts as strike us as remarkable, if possible to explain their nature, to compare it with the nature of other interesting facts, and to see whether, in this fashion, we can gradually discover general rules which hold for many phenomena. Obviously, in this program the local simple elements or sensations were never mentioned. For this reason and for others, the Gestalt psychologists were soon suspected of being mystics. We will now see what these "mystics" achieved.

Mystery number one. The first psychologist who worked in this manner, and thus became the first Gestalt psychologist, was Max Wertheimer. He found one phenomenon, so-called stroboscopic or apparent movement, most interesting. Others who were acquainted with it had not been able to handle it in a psychologically productive fashion. The phenomenon as such is quite simple. When a visual object, for example a line, is shown briefly in one place and almost immediately afterwards a second object or line appears in a second place, not too distant, an observer does not see two objects appearing in quick succession at their two places; rather he sees one object moving rapidly from the first to the second place.

Stroboscopic movement may be demonstrated in a simple manner (Figure 1). Two electric lamps are placed behind a translucent screen, with a straight vertical rod midway between them, nearer to the screen than the lamps. A double switch makes it possible to turn the two lights on and off in rapid alternation. When the one lamp is switched on, a shadow of the rod appears on one part of the screen, while the other lamp casts a shadow in a different place. Physically, when one light is turned off, the corresponding shadow simply disappears. Physically, therefore, when one lamp is turned on, then turned off and the other switched on, no more can happen than that the first shadow appears and disappears in one place, and then the second shadow appears and disappears in another place. Surely no physical movement occurs from one place to the other. Actually, when the shadows are made to appear and disappear in a rapid sequence, one shadow will be seen moving back and forth across the screen.

Figure 1

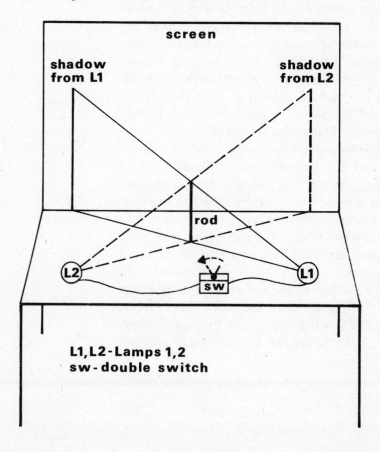

screen

shadow from L1

shadow from L2

rod

L2

sw

L1

L1, L2 - Lamps 1,2
sw - double switch

Wertheimer investigated the special conditions under which this phenomenon appears. Others had not done so, because they felt that stroboscopic or apparent movement was simply an *illusion*, not only because it did not agree with the physical facts before the observer, but also because it disagreed with the thesis that perceptual facts consist of "independent local sensations." What did the term "illusion" mean? It meant that stroboscopic movement was not accepted as a perceptual fact at all; it was held to be the product of a mistake in the observer's thinking. Two equal perceptual facts seen in such a rapid succession, it was said, are erroneously identified by the observer, and this leads to the illusion that a single object moves from one place to the other.

Since nobody tried to discover whether this was really the right explanation of the observed movement, the explanation remained a mere excuse, an "explaining away" of the disturbing observation. "Explaining away" was at the time done over and over again by those who did not like the Gestalt psychologists' observations or other facts that disturbed the belief in "independent local sensations" as the real content of perceptual fields. Even at the present time, the art of "explaining away" has not entirely disappeared from psychology and probably makes this young science more conservative and less productive than it would be if surprising observations aroused more interest and then led to closer investigation of such facts rather than to attempts to get rid of the disturbances.

Wertheimer did not make this mistake. He quietly examined apparent movement in many experiments. Let me mention at least one of his findings which seems to me to be entirely incompatible with the assumption that apparent movement is no more than an illusory product of careless judging.

When an ordinary (or real) movement has occurred over and over again in a given part of the visual field, an observer who has watched the repeated displacements for some time and now looks at any visual scene which is physically at rest immediately sees in this scene a movement in the direction opposite to the one of the previously watched displacements. This is called a negative after image of the movement seen before. Wertheimer (and independently the physiologist Exner) saw a problem here. Under optimal conditions, a so-called apparent and a corresponding real movement look exactly alike; when the two movements occur side by side, people cannot decide which is the "merely apparent" and which the "real" movement. Continued observation of an "apparent" movement might therefore also be followed by a negative after image. The experiment was done by both Exner and Wertheimer, and it was a complete success. Apparent movement, too, was visually followed by a movement in the opposite direction. According to this test, so-called apparent movement is, as a perceptual fact, just as real as a so-called real movement.

Most of us here know that the objects shown in the films of a movie theater never move while the individual pictures of the film are actually shown on the screen. One picture is rapidly replaced by the next; during the change no light is projected on the screen. Consequently the film consists of a physical sequence of many different pictures at rest. The movements which the audience sees are therefore all apparent or stroboscopic movements. It would not be easy to convince the audience that, actually, no real movements ever occur on the screen, and that the movements which they seem to see are mere consequences of thousands of mistaken judgments within a few minutes.

But if apparent movement is perceptually real, then it clearly proves that, when local stimulations occur in different places under certain temporal conditions, the corresponding visual processes are by no means independent local facts; rather, these processes *interact*, and thus the traditional axiom that they must be independent local facts has to be discarded. This was the view briefly formulated by Wertheimer. Unfortunately, at the time it was impossible to tell precisely what kind of interaction was involved. And so, in a sense, apparent movement still remained a mystery.

I have used apparent movement as a good first example of the Gestalt psychologists' interests and procedures. After this example, discussions of further Gestalt investigations can be kept much shorter.

The Gestalt psychologists now began to investigate a number of other problems. One such investigation, done in Kurt Koffka's laboratory, referred to a further puzzle in the field of visual movement, so-called gamma movement. When an object suddenly appears in the visual field, this object rapidly expands, and when the object suddenly disappears, it contracts. Similarly, when not one object but a group of objects is suddenly shown, the members of this group rapidly move away from each other so that the whole group expands. Here again, we ask ourselves: How, if the individual figures are independent local facts, is the expansion of the group to be explained? Why do the individual figures move away from each other? Again, we are confronted with an interaction, but now an interaction which has the character of a mutual repulsion of the individual figures. Once more, this fact is incompatible with the view that local items in the perceptual field are independent of what appears in their environment. But why, in the present case, the case of a gamma movement, has the interaction the character of a repulsion? It was, of course, impossible to answer this question at the time. Only now, many years later, are we beginning to understand such observations.

The Gestalt psychologists' next question was whether interactions of this kind occur only in the case of movement. Are there also observations which demonstrate the dependence of local facts upon conditions in their environment when the observed perceptual objects remain at rest? The answer to this question was extremely simple. No new discoveries were needed; such facts had been known for a long time. Take color vision: when a gray object surrounded by a white surface is compared with a second object that, physically, has the same gray color but is surrounded by a black surface, the gray-on-white object looks darker than the gray-on-black object. Similar effects of the color of the environment on a local color can also be demonstrated when the surrounding colors in question are so-called hues, that is, red or yellow or green or blue. In a red environment, for instance, a gray object tends to look greenish, and so forth. Well known though such examples of simultaneous brightness and color contrast were, they had (just like apparent movement) often been "explained away" as mere consequences of erroneous judging—because they were also incompatible with the thesis that local visual facts are independent facts. Now, when psychologists began to realize that such an "explaining away" of obvious perceptual phenomena could no longer be accepted as a legitimate procedure, color contrast had naturally to be regarded as further proof that the properties of local facts are affected by the conditions present in their environment, in other words, that interaction takes place in the perceptual field.

I now turn to a further group of facts which prove the same thing. These facts are the so-called geometrical illusions, a veritable crowd of distortions of visual shapes by certain other shapes in their environment. Most of us are probably familiar with certain phenomena of this kind. I will therefore confine myself to two particularly striking examples taken from an old issue of the *British Journal of Psychology*. The drawings are made up of objectively very accurately constructed circles. But these circles are surrounded by certain other patterns, and as a consequence the perceptual counterparts of the objective circles are no longer circles. For instance, Figure 2 almost looks like a square. Figure 3, which consists physically of a number of concentric circles, has the appearance of

a spiral. But these spiral-like curves are physically closed, as may be demonstrated by following them with a pencil or compass.

Enough of such striking geometrical illusions or distortions. You will not be sur-

Figure 2. From J. B. Fraser, A new visual illusion of direction, *British Journal of Psychology* 2 (1908).

Figure 3. From *British Journal of Psychology* 2 (1908).

prised to hear that these observations, too, were generally considered to be consequences of mere erroneous judgments, the observer being misled in his interpretation of what he sees by the background patterns. Why? The real perceptual facts *had* to be independent local facts, and their arrangement in space *had* to be determined by the geometrical arrangement of the corresponding physical facts. If any observation did not agree with this conviction, then the disagreement *had* to be "explained away" in the way I have just mentioned.

For some reason, the early Gestalt psychologists paid little attention to these illusions as such and to the somewhat fantastic interpretation of such facts as mere errors of judgment. But they should have paid attention, because such geometric illusions are excellent demonstrations of the fact that, when certain patterns are brought together in a visual field, their perception may be distorted by very strong interactions. This means, of course, that when the psychologist tries to understand what happens in perception, his observations must, from the very beginning, refer to fairly large wholes, within which such distorting interactions take place. But no! Ebbinghaus, the psychologist who first showed how certain forms of human learning can be studied in simple experiments, made the following surprising remark: "I am not sure whether psychological facts are merely aggregates of psychological atoms; but, being scientists, we must proceed as though this were true." What a sad statement. It seems to tell us that certain alleged necessities of scientific procedure are more important than the nature of the facts that we investigate, with the consequence that we may ignore such facts as seem to be at odds with those "scientific necessities."

Several years earlier, another psychologist, Christian von Ehrenfels in Austria, found himself confronted with the same difficulty. He was not yet interested in the question of whether certain psychological facts must be regarded as consequences of interactions among parts of perceptual fields. Rather, he merely called our attention to almost omnipresent properties of objects in such fields— properties which seem entirely unrelated to the properties of the postulated elementary local stimulations and sensations. Our sensory fields, he said, may contain numerous simple sensations which are all related to specific local stimuli and are therefore mutually independent elements of such fields. But, he added, other characteristics of the same fields do not fit into this simple scheme. Take a melody or a musical chord. The melody, as we hear it, remains practically unchanged as a melody when the objective pitches are all shifted upward or downward in the same proportion so that only the relations remain unchanged. This also holds for musical chords. But perhaps the most obvious examples are the shapes which appear in visual fields. Such shapes may be reduced in size or enlarged; they may be shown in one part of the field or another, and their color may also be changed: all these variations hardly affect the perceptual character of the shapes as such—again, so long as the spatial relations among their parts remain the same. Now, the German word for shape is *Gestalt.* Thus, von Ehrenfels, giving the name of the most obvious example to all such characteristics, introduced the term Gestalt qualities. Gestalt qualities in this sense occur everywhere in perception. Even a whole visual field, for instance, may look "clear," and another almost "chaotic"; and even more important: the movements of one person are seen as "steady," those of another as "erratic"; the faces of some individuals impress us as relaxed, those of others as tense or keen or empty or soft, and so forth. Some such Gestalt qualities play a most important rôle among the aesthetic characteristics of our perceptual environment and, naturally, also in the products of artists.

Von Ehrenfels too was disturbed by the fact that his Gestalt qualities did not fit into the traditional scheme of scientific thinking, according to which one has first of all to analyze perceptual scenes in order to discover their elements and thus their true nature. Some of the Gestalt qualities which I have just mentioned even Ehrenfels might have refused to accept as perceptual facts. But he had no doubts as to the perceptual nature of the characteristic shapes of objects or the fascinating properties of melodies and chords. Clearly, the dependence of such perceptual characteristics upon the relations among individual stimulating facts rather than on these facts taken singly cannot possibly be denied, and thus the atomism assumedly necessary in psychology was again shown to be a mistaken conception.

Although this is a sound argument, it is unfortunately a merely negative argument. It shows that one particular interpretation of perceptual fields cannot explain a great many obvious properties of perception; but the Gestalt psychologists of that time could not suggest a better interpretation. It will be remembered that, when we discussed other perceptual facts in which the Gestalt psychologists were interested, the result of their work was always the same. Their findings were always incompatible with the atomistic conceptions accepted by other psychologists, but they offered no positive explanatory principle in any case, not when they studied apparent movement, not in the case of gamma movement, not in that of color contrast, and not in that of the geometrical illusions. Now, do we achieve enough in science if we find certain facts most interesting, but then say only that a widely accepted assumption is unable to explain them? The Gestalt psychologists were clearly fascinated by their remarkable findings; they found them far more attractive than the local sensations traditionally regarded as *the* perceptual material. But were the Gestalt psychologists perhaps also attracted by the fact that nobody could explain these findings and that, in this sense, their observations remained mysteries? Once in a conversation, the late Karl Lashley, one of the most important psychologists of the time, told me quietly, "Mr. Köhler, the work done by the Gestalt psychologists is surely most interesting. But sometimes I cannot help feeling that you have religion up your sleeves." I do not know whether a certain elation among scientists who feel that they have arrived at a turning point in their field is a religious feeling. But surely, Gestalt psychologists did not object to adequate attempts to discover precisely what processes brought about their remarkable phenomena. When later the real nature of these processes became gradually known, Wertheimer, Koffka, and the present speaker simply enjoyed what was happening.

However, this development had not yet begun when Gestalt psychology took its first step—and this step seemed even more disturbing to other psychologists. So far, the Gestalt psychologists had been interested in some strange perceptual experiences. But now Wertheimer turned to perceptual facts which are present in practically all visual fields and had, therefore, simply been taken for granted by everybody. He showed that these familiar facts were actually just as unexplained and remarkable as apparent movement, the Gestalt qualities, and so forth. To the opponents this meant, of course, that from now on they were supposed to regard practically everything in perception as a mystery. Wertheimer asked the following question: If it is assumed that the visual field consists of local elements, the sensations, where *are* these local elements? Has anybody ever told us that, to him, the visual field appears as a mosaic of such little pieces? If we never hear such statements, what is the empirical foundation of the atomistic thesis in our field? What people actually mention when they refer to contents of their visual environment are mostly visual objects: glasses, plates, tables, chairs, houses, trees, other people, dogs, cats, and so on. All these objects are parts of the visual field, but, far from being tiny elements, they are for the most part fairly large unitary entities or "wholes." In a first attempt to study perception, would it not be a more empirical procedure if one started with these obvious visual facts rather than with the hypothetical mosaic of local sensations? The opponents did not like to hear the word "wholes" again. "We do not want to hear more about mysteries," they would say. "We want to hear, rather, how you explain the existence of your 'object-wholes.' We do not deny that people talk about such objects. But we have a simple explanation of this common tendency. From early childhood, the human being becomes acquainted with the fact that certain regions of the perceptual mosaic move together, can be handled as units, and in this practical sense behave as though they were unitary entities. Such practical experiences are impressed on the child's memory; consequently, when the same regions of the mosaic appear again, the earlier experiences of their unitary behavior are recalled, and, as a result, those regions now look as though they were molar perceptual units." Wertheimer was aware of the fact that sometimes previous experiences do influence the way a visual scene looks. But, for good reasons, he refused to accept the opponents' use of this fact as an explanation of our ordinary perception of molar objects or "things." These were his reasons:

We often see visual entities with which we are not acquainted, which we do not recognize, and which we can therefore not

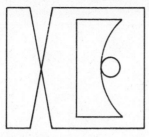

Figure 4

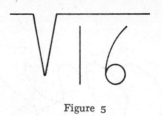

Figure 5

have learned to regard as such unitary entities. This happens, for instance, when we are in a room or a landscape which is only dimly lighted. "What is that dark thing over there?" we may then say. And yet, at the same time, that unknown part of the field is surely seen as a molar unit. Nor is this the only way of showing that past experience cannot be the main factor that makes us see unitary objects or things. Figure 4, particularly when it is presented in a rather short exposure, usually gives the impression of a pattern that is not at all familiar. But it contains one part with which we are all well acquainted; this part is shown in Figure 5. What does this prove? It proves that the causes which really establish unitary visual things may operate in a way that makes well-known objects disappear, because they are not visually separated from perfectly unknown larger entities which we *do* see. Clearly, therefore, the principles according to which visual objects are established differ from the processes which the empiristic explanation, the explanation of learning, makes one expect.

51

Figure 6

Figure 6 illustrates the same point; it appears at first as an unknown total pattern, which might perhaps be described as a horizontal row of forms resembling hearts. But this pattern contains a very simple and extremely well-known word, not immediately perceived, namely the word "men." To the upper part of the pattern, the word "men," its mirror image is simply added as the lower part. Now, the processes responsible for the formation of visual objects tend to form closed figures rather than mere linear patterns. Thus a row of less known, closed figures is seen spontaneously; it absorbs the mere lines of the word and therefore makes this word disappear. One can easily construct hundreds of patterns in which the same thing happens. Well-known objects are not seen, because the processes really active in forming visual entities often operate against the appearance of the familiar objects.

The facts which we have just discussed prove not only that past experience cannot be the main factor responsible for the appearance of objects in visual fields. Our observations also indicate that, when referring to such objects, one should not simply call them "wholes." Surely, they *are* wholes rather than mere regions within a general mosaic of local sensations. But we should always add an adjective, namely "segregated" or "detached" wholes. For we have just seen that objects appear in the visual field only if their boundaries are visually preserved. Consequently, the processes which make visual objects emerge in the field are just as much processes which establish certain separations, separations of visual units, as they are processes which make objects unitary entities. This aspect of what we now call "perceptual organization" was not always sufficiently emphasized in early Gestalt psychology.

I continue my discussion of Wertheimer's work. He was, of course, aware of the fact that there are extended units not only in quiet visual fields but also in sequences of perceptual events. For instance, the words, the sentences, and the melodies which we hear are such extended wholes. Next, Wertheimer realized that the Gestalt qualities of which von Ehrenfels had spoken were for the most part characteristics of specific perceptual wholes. This is obviously true of visual shapes but also of Gestalt qualities present in music. Thus the Gestalt qualities which the musicians call "major" and "minor" are characteristics of musical phrases rather than of individual tones. The problem that von Ehrenfels had raised was, therefore, part of this more general problem: Why are there, both in space and in time, such molar entities? This was the problem that Wertheimer tried to solve.

Incidentally, quite apart from Ehrenfels' Gestalt qualities, we find further interesting facts in segregated molar entities and only in such entities. I will call these facts "dependent part qualities," because they owe their appearance to the rôle which they play in such wholes. In a melody, for instance, a certain pitch is called the tonic. It is heard as a kind of resting point in the melody. Clearly, this property of a tone depends upon its position within the melody. For, if the melody is transposed to another level of the scale, another pitch acquires, and the former tonic loses, its character as a resting point.

Other dependent qualities appear in simple visual perception. For instance, when we look at the molar unit which is called a square, four points in the boundary of this figure have the character of being "corners." Precisely the same points in the same locations would not have this particular character if they were points of the boundary of a circle. Being a corner is, therefore, not a property which these points have as such; rather, it is a property which they acquire within a particular larger context.

A contemporary of the early Gestalt psychologists, Rubin in Denmark, called attention to a further phenomenon that accompanies the segregation of a visual object from its environment. Even when this object is physically perfectly flat, and lies in the same physical plane as its environment, it is, as a percept, slightly raised; it is located *in front* of the environment. Rubin could not know this, but at the present time his observation seems to become quite important for our understanding of visual depth in general.

In the meantime, Wertheimer had extended his observations in a most radical fashion. In visual space (but also in other perceptual fields) individual unitary objects often become parts of larger perceptual units which are commonly called "groups." When this happens, one often observes effects on this new higher level of unification that are like those I just mentioned when discussing the properties of individual objects. A simple example: when a large number of small circles are given the right places relative to each other, this assembly of segregated figures appears as a square; in other words, one of Ehrenfels' Gestalt qualities is now seen as a property of the whole group of spatially separated objects. Moreover, within this group, certain members again acquire "dependent part qualities," qualities which they owe to their location within the larger entity: thus four of the little circles involved are now seen as "corners" of the square-group. Trivial though such facts may appear to the layman, in the further development of Gestalt psychology they have proved to be fairly important, particularly after Wertheimer had investigated many varieties of grouping.

The formation of larger unitary entities, the groups, out of individual segregated units, the appearance of Gestalt qualities and of dependent part qualities in such groups, may seem merely to be further mysteries of the kind in which the early Gestalt psychologists were said to be strangely interested. How can such things happen when the members of a group are separated often by considerable distances? What processes would be able to achieve such curious effects? Actually, however, Wertheimer found it easier to formulate simple descriptive principles which govern the *grouping* of segregated objects than to discover such principles in the case of individual coherent objects.

A *first* principle: Although grouping may occur when the distances between the member-objects are considerable, the grouping is facilitated when the distances are smaller. Moreover, when a number of individual objects are nearer to one another than they are to other objects in the environment, then not one but two such groups tend to be formed, as in Figure 7.

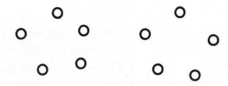

Figure 7

A *second* principle: Similarity of the individual objects as to shape or color, or both, facilitates their appearance as one group. But again, when some of the individual objects are similar or equal in such properties, while further objects, again similar or equal to one another, have other shapes or colors, then the whole assembly tends to *split*, that is, to appear as a combination of two subgroups (Figure 8).

A *third* principle: When individual objects form groups or sub-groups, such groups or sub-groups tend to be established as are, *qua* groups, particularly simple, symmetrical, and smooth. One is tempted to say that, in such instances, the direction of the group-

Figure 8

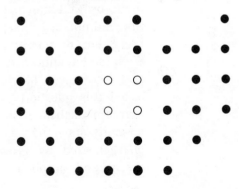

ing coincides with a direction often recognized in simplest aesthetics. Incidentally, Wertheimer discovered that this principle is followed not only in the case of grouping, but sometimes also in the formation of simpler individual coherent perceptual objects. Moreover, the principle seems to operate in a most convincing fashion when apparent movements and similar phenomena occur repeatedly in a given place: often the form of the movements and the shape of the moving objects may then change, and such changes always seem to occur in the direction of greatest simplicity and regularity.

Does this seem to be the greatest mystery ever encountered in an enterprise that claims to be a science? We have just arrived at a quite important point in our consideration of perceptual facts. This is not a mystery at all. Wertheimer's third principle, which may at first have sounded so strange, is practically identical with statements repeatedly made by well-known physicists, who at the time did not, of course, refer to psychological facts, but to purely physical observations. Such statements come from Pierre Curie and from Ernst Mach. Mach, for instance, asked this question: When a physical system approaches a state of equilibrium or a steady state, why is this change so often characterized by growing regularity, symmetry, and simplicity in the distribution of the material and the forces within the system? There seems to be a very simple answer. When such regular distributions are being established, more and more components of the acting forces are likely to balance each other, which means that under these circumstances the equilibrium or a steady state is quickly or gradually approached. But in a closed system the action of forces does operate in the direction of equilibrium or a steady state. It is therefore not surprising that during this operation the distributions within the system become more regular, symmetrical and simple.[1]

This is an over-simplified explanation of the direction toward symmetry and regularity which occurs so often in physical systems when they approach a quiet state. Ernst Mach has given a much more adequate explanation in slightly more abstract, but precise, terms.

Clearly, therefore, the early Gestalt psychologists were not wrong when they trusted their observations which appeared so mysterious to other psychologists. For now the Gestalt psychologists discovered that this procedure made them neighbors of the most advanced natural scientists, the physicists.

But this was not all. Several years later I discovered that some eminent physicists agreed with the Gestalt psychologists' scientific procedure in a much more general sense.

[1] Cf. E. Mach. *Die Mechanik in ihrer Entwickelung.* 3rd edn., 1897. Pp. 389-390.

At the time I was studying the writings of two such physicists, Clerk Maxwell, the greatest figure in the development of field physics, and Max Planck, the physicist who first introduced the concept of the quantum in physics.

In the introduction to his *Treatise on Electricity and Magnetism*, Maxwell compared the methods of Faraday with those then current in mathematical physics. The methods of Faraday, Maxwell explained, resembled those in which one begins with a given "whole," and only then arrives at the parts by analysis, while the ordinary procedures are founded on the principle of beginning with the parts and building up the wholes by synthesis.[2] Maxwell made it quite clear that he preferred Faraday's way, that of proceeding from the given wholes to the parts. Again, in the same treatise, the author remarks, "We are accustomed to consider the universe as made up of parts, and mathematicians usually begin by considering a single particle, and then conceiving its relation to another particle, and so on. This has generally been supposed the most natural method. To conceive of a particle, however, requires a process of abstraction, since all our perceptions are related to extended bodies, so that the idea of the *all* that is in our consciousness

[2] J. C. Maxwell. *A Treatise on Electricity and Magnetism.* Oxford: Clarendon Press, 1873. Vol. 1, pp. x-xi.

at a given instant is perhaps as primitive an idea as that of any individual thing."[3]

When Maxwell made these statements, he was, of course, not influenced by any Gestalt psychologists. The statement that I just quoted was written in 1873, almost forty years before the Gestalt psychologists began their work.

I next read a book of Max Planck's lectures delivered in 1909 in New York City. In one of these lectures, Planck discusses the concept of irreversible processes, a concept which plays a central rôle in what the physicists call the Second Principle of Thermodynamics. In this connection, the author makes the following statement:

> In physics, it is our habit to try to approach the explanation of a physical process by splitting this process into elements. We regard all complicated processes as combinations of simple elementary processes, . . . that is, we think of the wholes before us as the sums of their parts. But this procedure presupposes that the splitting of a whole does not affect the character of this whole. . . . Now, when we deal with irreversible processes in this fashion, the irreversibility is simply lost. One cannot understand such processes on the assumption that all properties of a whole may be approached by a study of its parts.

[3] *Ibid.*, Article 529. Vol. 2, p. 163.

Planck adds the following extraordinary sentence: "It seems to me that the same difficulty arises when we consider most problems of mental life."[4]

Eddington, too, wrote, "There is one ideal of survey which would look into each minute compartment of space in turn to see what it may contain and so make what it would regard as a complete inventory of the world. But this misses any world-features which are not located in minute compartments."[5]

My quotations, I hope, have made it clear that, far from proceeding in a fantastic fashion, the early Gestalt psychologists (at the time not yet acquainted with these remarkable statements of great scientists) almost naïvely worked in a direction which entirely agreed with tendencies that had emerged in natural science.

Under the circumstances, it is not surprising if I next discuss basic concepts of natural science, not only of physics but also of biology. For some concepts of physics and of biology must be clearly understood if serious errors are to be avoided.

[4] M. Planck. *Acht Vorlesungen über Theoretische Physik*. Leipzig: S. Hirzel, 1910. Pp. 96-97. Cf. also the English translation: *Eight Lectures on Theoretical Physics*. Trans. by A. P. Wills. New York: Columbia University Press, 1915. Pp. 97-98.

[5] A. S. Eddington. *The Nature of the Physical World*. New York: Macmillan; and Cambridge: The University Press, 1929. P. 103.

II · GESTALT PSYCHOLOGY AND NATURAL SCIENCE

In the previous lecture I said that, until about 1920, the Gestalt psychologists did not often look beyond their psychological observations, which referred to interesting facts in perception. I added that they were unable to explain their findings in this field. For instance, the fact that, under certain conditions, the mere sequence of two objects shown in different places is transformed into the movement of one object—across the space between them—does not tell the observer why this happens. Similarly, during observations of striking geometrical illusions, one merely sees amazing distortions, but one does not see why the shapes of given simple patterns are radically altered by patterns which surround them, and so forth.

The Gestalt psychologists suspected that such phenomena are caused by interactions, but they could not yet tell why such interactions occurred, that is, what forces or processes were involved. Perception only showed the effects of such hypothetical causes; it told the observer nothing about the nature of these causes. The forces and processes which underlie such perceptual facts are simply not represented in the phenomenal, the perceptual, world.

Now, there is only one part of the world the processes of which are in close contact with the perceptual experiences of the human being and which may therefore determine the character of these experiences. Hence, the Gestalt psychologists had to assume that the unknown events responsible for such curious interactions in perceptual fields were processes in the corresponding parts of the human brain, mainly in the gray cover of the brain, the cortex. We know from pathological cases, and from other evidence, where in the brain the processes directly related to vision take place, also where the physiological correlates of our hearing, where those of our tactual experiences are located, and so forth. But our main question is, of course, what physiological events occur in these places when human beings have perceptual experiences of one kind or another. Wilhelm Wundt, the psychologist who is often regarded as the founder of experimental psychology, gave this radical answer: "Brain processes and corresponding psychological facts differ entirely as to the nature of both their elements and of the connections among these elements." Now, when we consider the previous lecture, we are likely to regard Wundt's statement as at least exaggerated. It will be recalled, for instance, that according to several physicists the distribution of materials and processes in physical systems tends to become regular, simple, and often symmetrical when the systems approach a state of equilibrium or a steady state. But, quite unaware of this behavior of physical systems, the early Gestalt psychologists discovered that the same rule holds also for developments in human perception. Why should such a similarity of the behavior of perceptual and physical facts become impossible when the physical facts in question happen to be physiological processes in the brain? I need not mention further examples which also suggest that sometimes the behavior of physical processes resembles that of psychological events. To be sure, human perception contains many facts the like of which never occur in the physical world. Take the sensory qualities in vision, such as blue, gray, yellow, green and red. In the physical world, the physicists find nothing that resembles these qualities, and nobody expects physiological processes in the visual cortex of the brain to have such characteristics. But we did not refer to sensory qualities when we began to suspect that certain properties of perceptual fields resemble properties of cortical processes to which they are related. The properties we had in mind were *structural* properties. If, for instance, under certain conditions, perceptual processes tend to assume particularly regular and simple forms, and if we suspect that, under the same conditions, corresponding processes in the brain show the same tendency, then we refer to what I just called "structural" characteristics. It is only such structural characteristics which, not only in this case but also in many others, perceptual facts and corresponding brain events may have in common.

In 1920, the Gestalt psychologists transformed this assumption into the following general hypothesis. Psychological facts and the underlying events in the brain resemble each other in all their structural characteristics. Today, we call this the hypothesis of Psychophysical Isomorphism.

I repeat: this is an hypothesis. Obviously, we can test it only if we add precisely what physical processes we assume to occur in human brains when the owners of these brains have structured experiences. As a matter of principle, it has not been too difficult to discover the nature of these processes. But we are still in danger of making serious mistakes when we try to apply our general hypothesis of isomorphism to specific phenomena in the psychological world. For this reason, I will now turn to biology and discuss some basic problems in this field with which we must be acquainted if we wish to give our hypothesis a more precise content.

Such basic problems are perhaps most clearly seen in connection with the views once expressed by a great philosopher, René Descartes, who about three hundred years ago also tried to explain the functions of the nervous system. In one respect, some present thinking about the nervous system still resembles that of Descartes, who at this point was seriously mistaken. It will be our first task to discuss this error.

Descartes, it will be recalled, was a strict dualist. The mind, he would say, has its characteristics and its laws, and so has the body. The characteristics and laws of the body differ entirely from those of the mind. Now, individual philosophers have held strictly dualistic views for various reasons. But mostly, mental processes appeared to them so far superior to the processes which occur in nature that, according to such authors, this fundamental difference must be emphasized all the time. These philosophers were dualists for the sake of the mind. Most probably this was also true of Descartes. Now, before Descartes, psychological concepts were by no means always regarded as being only psychological. Rather, some such concepts played a great rôle also in early biology, because certain facts in biology looked as though they were probably governed by principles similar to those governing psychological events. Descartes had no patience with such views. According to him, the body was a machine, and therefore psychological notions had to be ignored when this mere machine was being investigated.

Now all this is not quite so clearly said in Descartes' own writings. In his time, a philosopher who liked to pursue his important studies without disturbance from the outside had to be pretty careful. Just outside the walls of Paris, the writings of Harvey, the discoverer of the circulation of the blood, had recently been burned in public. According to traditional views, a creature of so much dignity as man could not possibly be a seat of permanent unrest, such as circulation of the blood. Really good things, it was thought, are always stable and solid. There was also the great unpleasantness to which Galileo was subjected because of his views in astronomy. When using his new telescope in observations of the planets and of the sun, he had found that here, too, there was quite a bit of complication and change, while the authorities knew for certain that, in the distinguished realm beyond the moon, everything occurred in a steady, simple, and harmonious fashion. Again, another philosopher, Giordano Bruno, had actually been burned at the stake for his unpopular views about the universe. Thus, for a while, Descartes kept some of his manuscripts hidden underground, and he would often describe his opinions as though they were somebody's fancies rather than his own convictions.

The interpretation of the human organism as a machine was, of course, also a shocking enterprise. Again, therefore, Descartes disguised his views by saying that he was merely concerned with a certain robot which resembled the human body in a most extraordinary fashion. Let me quote a few paragraphs from his treatise *De l'Homme* and from another work, *Les Passions de l'Âme*. In my translations, I have transformed some of Descartes' baroque periods into several shorter sentences. Nowhere, however, have I changed the meaning of Descartes' original statements.

Once Descartes addresses the reader as follows:

I wish you would realize that all functions which I attribute to this machine of mine follow quite naturally from the way in which its "organs" are connected and arranged—just as the movements of a clock or another automaton follow from the arrangement of certain weights and wheels. This holds for the way in which our machine digests, in which its heart and blood vessels pulsate, in which it breathes, is awake or sleeps; it holds for the stimulation of its external sense organs by light, sound, odor, taste, heat and the like; for the retention of such impressions in memory, and also for the inner stirrings which are called appetites and passions. Finally, it is again true of the external movements of its members. To such a degree are these movements of the machine in line with the actions of outside objects, and also with the passions, and the impressions stored in memory, that the "imitation of a real human being" is about as perfect as it could be. Obviously, in understanding the machine, it is not necessary to refer to a special vegetative or sensitive soul-like principle. We have to refer only to the blood and to the animal spirits which are agitated by the permanent heat in the heart; and this heat is, of course, of exactly the same kind as the heat found in any inanimate objects.[1]

In passing, let us remember that the soul-like vegetative and sensitive principles mentioned and rejected by Descartes were favorite biological concepts of certain Greek philosophers, and later of some Scholastic schools; we must also remember that there is nothing spiritual about the "animal spirits" (*esprits animaux*) which Descartes accepts. They play only the rôle of an extremely thin fluid, or gas, which is heated by the heart.

Descartes next considers the nervous system. There, he says, we have an ensemble of containers and tubes in which this fluid, the

[1] *Traité de l'Homme*, Article 106. (Article numbers are those added by Clerselier in the 1664 edition.)

animal spirits, is stored or circulates. Where are these containers? At this point, the author develops a most extraordinary thesis. While we regard the tissue of the brain as most essential, for Descartes this tissue mainly constitutes the walls around the really relevant containers, and these containers are what we call the ventricles, certain spaces surrounded by brain tissue and actually filled with cerebrospinal fluid. But, in Descartes' neurology, these ventricles are of paramount importance, because they contain the animal spirits, the material which makes the human machine move. I quote again: "There are pores in the walls of the cerebral containers, through which the animal spirits can pass into the nerves; and depending upon what pores and what nerves they enter in a given instance, they can then change the shape of the muscles in which the nerves end, so that the members of the machine move[2]—just as the air in a balloon makes the balloon expand and grow hard." After this surprising aerodynamical interpretation of muscle action, Descartes makes the following remark:

Such things are, of course, known to you from the artificial grottos and waterworks in the gardens of our kings, where the mere power of water, as it escapes from its source, suffices for throwing one device or another into action, or even for making

[2] *Ibid.*, Article 15.

certain instruments play music, or others pronounce a few words—entirely according to the arrangement of the pipes which connect the source with these devices.[3] Surely, one can compare the nerves of our machine with such pipes, and its muscles and tendons with the devices and springs in such water-driven artifacts, and the animal spirits with this water itself. Furthermore, the outside objects which in our machine affect the sense organs, and thus indirectly cause muscular activities,—they are just like visitors who happen to approach one of those grottos or waterworks, and unawares step upon certain plates hidden in the ground, whereupon the statue of a Diana, who is just getting ready for a bath, rapidly retires into the surrounding bushes, and when they try to follow, and now step upon another plate, a Neptune moves threateningly toward them with his trident, or a sea monster spits water right into their faces. Of course, if a reasonable soul were now placed in our machine, in the middle of its brain, it would there play the rôle of the man who is responsible for such waterworks, and must therefore stay in their very center, the place from which the various pipes diverge toward the special devices which I have just mentioned.[4]

[3] *Ibid.*, Article 15.
[4] *Ibid.*, Article 16.

One more point, and we know enough about Descartes' neurology. He does not assume that transmission in nerves is exclusively a matter of the animal spirits which move along these pipe-like conductors. This, he believes, happens only when our muscles are thrown into action, that is, when nerve transmission occurs toward the periphery. Transmission in the opposite direction, which is caused by peripheral stimulation, follows a different principle. In the middle of each nerve tube there is a thread which extends from a sense organ to the central end of the tube in the brain. Stimulation somewhere in a sense organ means that one such thread is slightly pulled, that this pull is transmitted along the thread up to the brain, and that, as a result, a certain pore in the wall of the ventricles is temporarily opened. Now, of course, some animal spirits escape into the tube or pipe, travel in the opposite direction, and blow up some muscle, so that we obtain what we now call reflex action, for instance, automatic withdrawal of a foot which has come too near a fire.[5]

Curiously enough, this strange picture of nerve action was widely accepted for a period of almost one hundred and fifty years, that is, until the latter part of the eighteenth century. Descartes' main notion, however, was that of the organism (and, more particularly, of

[5] *Ibid.*, Article 26.

the nervous system) as a *machine*, and, in this essential respect, present views are often almost as Cartesian as though the philosopher lived among us and had merely substituted modern details for those which were plainly wrong in his original construction. Hence, if we now turn to the concept of a machine, and examine from the point of view of physics what this term means, we begin a discussion which concerns the present time no less than the views of a special historical period and of a particular person. What is a machine? The term is used in one sense by some authors and in a different sense by others. All systems in which processes are determined by given causes are sometimes called "machines." Even the physical universe as a whole has been given this name, merely on the assumption that all events in it are so determined. But the word "machine" has also a far more specific meaning, and it is in this special meaning that the machine concept has become so extremely important in biology. I must therefore try to make it clear that machines in this sense (which was also Descartes' sense) are extremely special.

The difference between typical machines and other systems in nature is perfectly clear in physics. Let us therefore consider very simple inanimate systems. Unless such systems are in a state of equilibrium, their parts are being displaced, for instance, by mutual *interaction*. This interaction and its effects we will call the dynamics of the system. For our present purpose, we will include in this dynamic category such actions as the pull of gravitation, electric and magnetic attractions and repulsions, electric currents, heat currents, currents of diffusion, chemical reactions, and so forth. So long as we ignore the most minute facts in nature, and deal only with major or so-called macroscopic systems, the general laws of dynamics are well known. So far, then, everything is quite elementary; and fortunately our next step will be equally simple.

A system may contain solid parts which are so rigid and so well fixed that they cannot be displaced, bent, or destroyed by dynamic actions in its interior. Such parts are not seriously disturbed by any dynamic events. These unalterable parts do, however, affect what happens in the system. For not all displacements which would occur if dynamics alone had to decide, can now actually take place. Rigid parts which are in the way of certain displacements either make these displacements entirely impossible, or else they permit only such components of dynamic action to be realized as are compatible with the position and the orientation of those rigid parts. The rigid parts of systems are called "constraints." An example: an object which we simply drop will move toward the earth in a straight vertical line. This is a case of dynamics unrestricted by constraints, of free dynamics. But if we place the same object on a smooth and rigid plane which has an oblique orientation in relation to the earth, the object can no longer simply follow the direction of gravitation. At every point, the gravitational component at right angles to the rigid surface is now eliminated, and only the component in line with the direction of the surface is left; in other words, the object will now follow the direction of the plane. Any rigid pipe in which water flows is another example of a constraint, because its solid walls prevent all movements of the water at right angles to the wall of the pipe. Naturally, if we give the pipe one form or another, the streaming fluid will be compelled to assume that form as the form of its own flow. All other possibilities are again excluded.

The degree to which the dynamics of a system is restricted by constraints may vary tremendously. Components of free dynamics may be eliminated only in a few places, or this elimination may go very far indeed. The most extreme case will be that of a system in which, everywhere, constraints exclude all components of dynamics excepting one. Under such conditions, the form of action in the system is entirely prescribed by the constraints. Any deviation from this form is made impossible by elimination of the components which would cause this deviation. When this extreme is reached, the system is a perfect machine; it realizes the very ideal of the type "machine." Machines in this sense of the term are most useful systems, or at least they may be useful if their constraints are properly chosen. Whenever man wants to achieve one particular form of dynamic action, and therefore to prevent any other form, a properly constructed machine will do just this for him. It is by the introduction of constraints that our various industries compel nature to do not what her free dynamics would do, but rather what is in line with some human purpose. To be sure, not all machines which are actually used in industry are perfect machines in our present theoretical sense, that is, systems with one possible mode of action only. In some, more than just one form of action is left possible. Steam engines, for instance, may have more than one—they may have two possible forms of action. It is customary to be liberal in the use of the term "machine," and to apply this name also to such systems, so long as their operations are useful. At any rate, between the theoretically ideal type of a machine and systems without any constraints there is a continuous series of intermediate systems.

At this point it is most important to remember that all systems, machines and the others, follow the general laws of physics and chemistry; in each, given conditions produce dynamic actions which can be predicted by the scientist. A system which is not a machine can be called free only inasmuch as it is free from constraints; in their absence, it merely becomes free to follow the principles inherent in its dynamics alone. On the other hand, even a machine in the strictest sense would not work at all if no components of dynamics were allowed to operate. Constraints as such cause no action whatsoever, they merely exclude some actions.

We can now return to Descartes' interpretation of the functions of the human organism, and more particularly to his curious neurology. I called this neurology a machine theory because he obviously derives orderly forms of action in the nervous system entirely from anatomical arrangements in the human body—which permit no other forms of action. These anatomical conditions are supposed to play the same part in the organism as solid restricting constraints play in our mechanical gadgets. It never occurred to Descartes that tendencies in dynamics as such could be responsible for orderly and useful events. We have seen that present neurology differs from Descartes' neurology in a great many other features. But it is still the main premise of much neurological thinking that the right, the orderly course of neural processes must throughout be prescribed by anatomical arrangements, that is, by constraints.

Now, is the human body a machine in the extreme sense that all its functions are compelled to take certain courses by corresponding anatomical constraints? The temptation to assume that this must be the case is surely very strong. At least this is the kind of explanation to which our thinking is most thoroughly accustomed. But I must at once admit that this is by no means a matter of human prejudice alone. Many anatomical facts simply are such that their rôle as useful constraints (by which functions are kept orderly) must be recognized by any objective observer. Even so, I suggest that we now assume a fairly cautious attitude, because explanations of orderly functions in such terms are surely not applicable to all biological situations. And I doubt whether they ever are complete explanations of what happens.

We are now gradually approaching problems that are just as important to the psychologist as they must be to the biologist. In fact, I make the following remarks about certain biological facts mainly because they will lead us to essential observations and questions in psychology.

Two familiar facts, both relevant to the life of all higher organisms, can surely not be explained in terms of special machine conditions. First, the distribution of certain materials in the organism is not completely regulated by such devices. For instance, the tissue fluid which we find in all tissues, which surrounds all cells, and which is, therefore, the medium in which they have to live, must have the right distribution if these cells are to survive. But there are hardly any special histological arrangements by which this right distribution of the tissue fluid is enforced. If, nevertheless, the right condition tends to be preserved (as it actually does), this must happen for what we have called purely dynamic reasons rather than because of anatomical constraints which would compel the fluid to be properly distributed. Seccondly, what has just been said about the tissue fluid is in a certain sense also true of the blood. The blood contains a great many chemicals, the delivery of which at one particular place or another is essential to the life of this or that tissue and of the organism. But in the blood vessels there are no special conductors for the various individual chemicals. Nonetheless, under normal conditions, these chemicals do arrive at their various right destinations. They must do so if life is to continue. But again, if they do, this must happen mainly for reasons inherent in dynamics, more particularly in chemical dynamics. What, then, is it in dynamics without constraints which makes it operate in this particular, highly selective, direction?

I am very much afraid of being misunderstood at this point. May I therefore repeat the following. When saying that certain biological facts cannot be explained in terms of special anatomical arrangements, that is, in machine terms, I am far from suggesting that such facts cannot be explained in terms of natural science. What I contrast is *not* Nature and Non-Nature (whatever that may be), but the basic forces and processes of nature as free to follow their inherent, dynamic, causally determined directions, and the same forces and processes almost or entirely compelled to take courses prescribed by constraints. If you want an example: no constraint compels a planet to move along its orderly orbit around the sun. The movement of the planet is an example of what I have called free dynamics. Nothing but the gravitational field operating between the sun and the planet is responsible.

I now turn to an issue that is even more basic to our main question. There is an altogether fundamental difference between the organism and (so far as I can tell) all manmade machines. Hardly any anatomical arrangement or constraint is an object (or a thing) in the sense in which the constraints of our machines are solid objects or things. The firm arrangements in these machines consist of given materials, just as a rock, or any piece of iron, contains the same solid material day after day, more probably year after year. It is precisely this solid material permanence of certain objects which we trust when we build the constraints of our machines. As soon as symptoms develop which indicate that the material of the constraints is no longer quite so solidly the same, we either discard the whole machine or replace the constraints in question by new pieces. But, to repeat, hardly any part of the organism, hardly any of its anatomical structures, is a solid object or thing in this sense. When closely examined, almost all these structures prove to be processes, so-called steady states, the materials of which are gradually and slowly being eliminated and, at the same time, replaced by metabolic activities. It is only the structures, the forms of these tissues, and the general kinds of material which they contain that do not vary. The individual molecules and so on, of which they consist, break down and disappear, while others, new specimens of the same substances, take their places, so that the histological forms of the structures are maintained. Now, in spite of this constant material change, in spite of the fact that anatomical structures are not permanent solid objects, these steady states are often so stable and tough that they can serve as constraints, by which more passing dynamic events in the organism are compelled to take certain courses. Hence, in a number of places, the organism can and does operate as though it were a machine. Even so, it is a most remarkable fact that, strictly speaking, there are hardly any "things" in the organism, that it consists almost entirely of processes. For, now the question arises why the various parts of an organism are for considerable periods maintained as certain forms, in spite of the fact that they are actually steady processes.

I now turn to the principle of evolution, because this principle is supposed to explain the way in which the various species have acquired their characteristic anatomy and corresponding functions. There seems to be no difficulty. Once there are small organisms with genes in their cells, and once we know that genes and gene systems tend to mutate, the familiar Darwinian thinking may—perhaps with some modern modifications—freely be used in the explanation of the origin of the various species.

But let us see what evolution *can* have done and what it can*not* possibly have done, if we accept the main postulate of modern evolutionary theory.

This is the postulate: all biological facts and events can be understood in terms of the laws which hold for facts and events in the inanimate world. In this respect, the principle of evolution is a principle of strict invariance rather than of change. As soon as entirely new laws, new elementary forces, and new elementary kinds of process are introduced in evolutionary theory, we can no longer properly speak of evolution. It is constancy in such matters which defines the very aim of evolutionary thinking—and which makes the principle of evolution so attractive to the scientist.

If the laws, the forces, and the elementary processes of inanimate nature are also to be those of living systems, what changes can evolution have produced? From the point of view of the physicist, which now must also be ours, there can be only one answer to this question: *via* gene situations, *via* subsequent changes in morphogenetic developments, and *via* corresponding selective actions of the environment, evolution must have introduced particular anatomical constraints. Constraints, we remember, do not themselves produce dynamic events; they merely eliminate certain dynamic components which would operate in the absence of the constraints. This must, of course, be true not only in inanimate systems but also in organisms. But if, in organisms, the elimination of certain dynamic components by constraints happens to cause forms of action which fit the environment better, then the organisms which are so equipped will survive longer, and will therefore have more offspring than others, and so forth.

No physicist, I hope, will object to this interpretation of evolution, particularly not to the implied assumption that processes in nature can establish constraints by their own occurrence. Surely, constraints may originate as direct results of dynamic events. For instance, in certain rectifiers, an electrolytically conducted current deposits on one electrode certain chemicals which at once react with the material of this electrode and here form an insulating cover. Thus the current itself establishes a new constraint which then compels this current to flow in a changed spatial distribution. Similarly, a physical process which occurs, say, in a just developing germ or embryo may there build a constraint which then compels the same or another process to take a somewhat changed course. Such biological assumptions remain, of course, entirely compatible with the laws of physics. Moreover, it will be remembered, the changed processes which must now occur also follow these laws. When a new constraint has been introduced, these laws still apply to the remaining dynamic events.

This must suffice as an extremely abbreviated and rough description of what physics and the principle of evolution permit or do not permit the evolutionist to postulate. No new laws, forces, or elementary processes are to be used in his thinking. Let us next enumerate the various events in living systems which require the present scheme—dynamics just as in the inanimate world plus constraints established by this dynamics itself. Apart from the developments which are supposed to have created first primitive living systems, the events which we have to consider are mainly mutations in genes and gene systems, morphogenetic developments, that is, the processes by which individual organisms grow from germ cells with given genes, and eventually the processes called functions which occur at one time or another when morphogenesis is more or less completed. This last class contains, of course, also the functions of the nervous system. Inasmuch as all facts in this list are processes and therefore dynamic events, the invariance of dynamics implied in the principle of evolution applies to the whole list. Thus, mutational changes in genes must follow laws of physics; morphogenesis, in spite of its tremendously complicated character, must be governed by laws which also hold for inanimate systems; all functions of the fully developed individual must be so governed; and finally this must again be true of all nervous processes, for instance of those which are directly related to psychological facts. Only if this condition is fulfilled can living rightly be called a stupendous amplification of physics and chemistry—and it must be fulfilled, if the theory of evolution is to deserve its name. But then it follows immediately that, according to this theory itself, an enormous part of the business of living can never, as such, have been affected by the changes introduced during evolution. To be sure, there have been such changes, namely, the development of innumerable new histological constraints, and in each case the corresponding elimination of certain dynamic components; but the events which are left must still occur according to the laws of the inanimate world, the world of physics, the fundamental dynamics of the world.

This may at first appear to be a trivial conclusion. But is it? Once, years ago, I studied some widely read books on evolution. The authors mostly began with the statement that, according to the principle of evolution, the laws of inanimate nature are valid throughout biology and suffice for explaining the anatomy and the functions of all living creatures, including man. This means, of course, the invariance principle in evolution. In later parts of the books, however, we hear only about mutations and about natural selection, while the fundamental premise of evolutionary theory, the postulate of invariance, is never mentioned again. In other words, the conclusion which we have just reached plays no part in the authors' further thinking about particulars in evolution. At the present time, I repeat, evolutionary theory is often freely applied to psychological facts, and to the processes in brains which accompany such facts. Now, some psychological facts occur as products of learning. For example, without having learned to do so, we could not read. On the other hand, some psychological facts owe virtually nothing to learning. For instance, the feeling of joy is not as such a product of learning, although some form of learning may connect it with particular situations. It is now universally accepted language to call the facts of the first class "acquired" or "learned," and those of the second class "inherited" or "innate." I have no objection to the first name; but the second name, "inherited," is not only ambiguous; often it is entirely misleading. For, quite apart from the question of whether these two classes can actually be so strictly separated, what exactly do we mean when we refer to an inherited or innate fact? We are right in speaking of inheritance when a person has blue rather than dark eyes. Again, there is something in the instinctive behavior of certain animals which can properly be called inherited. But what about the following fact? If, for one reason or another, the concentration of a certain chemical differs from one part of the tissue fluid to surrounding parts, diffusion will at once begin to equalize the concentration. This is dynamics; under comparable conditions the same process would occur everywhere in inanimate nature. What have the genes to do with this? And what inheritance? Again, do processes in our nervous system follow the laws of nature because some genes compel such processes to do so? And, in the absence of these genes, would other laws be followed? Obviously, such concepts as genes, inherited, and innate should never be mentioned when we refer to the basic, purely dynamic phase of processes in nervous systems. For, if we use these concepts in the present connection, we implicitly violate the main premise of evolutionary theory, namely, that evolution, genes, inheritance, and so on never really change dynamics as such. By the mere juxtaposition of the terms "learned" and "inherited," as though these words indicated an "either-or" alternative, we commit the same mistake. It is three factors by which events in organisms, and therefore also in nervous systems, are generally determined. First, the invariant principles and forces of general dynamics, secondly, anatomical constraints which evolution has established, and thirdly, learning. Under no circumstances should we forget that any processes in our brains, including those which go with psychological facts, must, *qua* processes, be realizations of universal dynamic laws, and to this extent be quite unrelated to evolution and inheritance. I repeat, this follows from the principle of evolution itself.

Why so much talk about inheritance, and so much about learning—but hardly ever a word about invariant dynamics? It is this invariant dynamics, however constrained by histological devices, which keeps organisms and their nervous systems going. I add an old quotation: *Hamlet*, it has been said, cannot be played without the Prince of Denmark. Why, then, are we consistently trying to do so on our stage?

We shall find the present critique of certain kinds of thinking in biology immediately relevant to our main task. It was our intention to discover what processes in the nervous system are related to the structural characteristics of human perception. The hypothesis of psychophysical isomorphism claims that the structural properties of these processes are the same as those of the corresponding perceptual facts. But this assumption will be acceptable only if we are actually able to find a specific physical process the behavior of which *might* be structured in this sense. In at least some cases this ought to be possible. Take this example—and now I repeat what I said in the beginning of the present lecture. In my first lecture I mentioned that early in the history of Gestalt psychology it was discovered that under certain conditions perceptual patterns show a tendency to assume particularly simple and regular structures. I added that, according to statements made by several physicists, in physical systems which approach steady states or equilibria, the distributions of materials and actions exhibit the same tendency. It seems reasonable to conclude that when perceptual distributions assume such regular and simple structures, the same happens to the distribution of the corresponding brain processes; in other words, that the perceptual facts show this tendency when the underlying physiological processes in the brain do so. This would be a specific case of isomorphism.

Now, in the examples mentioned by the physicists, developments occur in the direction of increasing simplicity and regularity for purely dynamic reasons. There are no special constraints in such physical systems which would compel the dynamic situations involved to behave in this fashion. Would it not be a curious coincidence if this were true in physics, while in the brain physiological events were compelled to follow the same rule by special constraints, constraints always properly arranged so as to force the brain processes to take this course? It is, therefore, our main task to find physical processes which occur in the brain and there tend, without constraints, to assume regular and simple distributions when corresponding perceptual patterns show this tendency. Before we approach this task, a further remark about what I called "structures" of physical events seems indicated. Sometimes the term "structure" is used in a purely geometrical sense. But when I use the term in our present connection, it refers to a functional aspect of processes, to the distribution of such processes, a distribution which they assume (and may also maintain) as a consequence of the dynamic interrelations or interactions among their parts. At this point, I must remind you of a statement of Max Planck which I mentioned earlier. The nature of irreversible processes, he said, can be understood only when we consider physical situations as wholes rather than as sums of their local parts. Unfortunately, Planck's example belongs to a rather difficult province of physics. Therefore, other examples now seem to me preferable. Take any cases of equilibria or of steady states in physics, for instance the distribution of an electric charge on an insulated conductor, say, a metallic ellipsoid. A very short time after the electric charge has arrived on that three-dimensional object, this charge is distributed on the surface of the object, and this functional distribution all over the surface is such that no forces are left which could produce further changes; it is an equilibrium distribution. Under these circumstances, can one understand why a particular spot on the surface has this or that particular charge by considering this spot by itself? This is entirely impossible; for, within the equilibrium, the spot has this particular charge only inasmuch as all other spots on this surface have *their* particular fitting charges, all of them together such that the distribution as a whole remains balanced. Precisely the same is true of the steady states which currents assume when flowing in a network of wires, as also in larger continuous conducting media. Everywhere in the system the intensity and direction of the local flow are such that the total distribution maintains itself unaltered. Again, therefore, one cannot understand what happens in a part of the conducting system without considering the distribution as a whole. Planck liked it very much when I once remarked that not only his example of irreversibility but many other simpler facts in physics clearly demonstrate that we have to consider the dynamic structures of whole processes or states when we wish to understand what happens in such physical systems.

Such examples have been introduced for a simple reason. What they tell us we have to apply to the dynamic structures of the physiological processes in the brain which are directly related to organized visual perception. These must be, in Maxwell's, in Planck's, and in my own sense, structured functional wholes.

III · RECENT DEVELOPMENTS IN GESTALT PSYCHOLOGY

In my first lecture I discussed what other psychologists called the "mysteries" investigated by the early Gestalt psychologists. And, to be sure, the Gestalt psychologists could not at the time explain what they were observing. Then, surprisingly, it was discovered that the main characteristic of such "mysteries" was well known to outstanding physicists, who described some problems in their own field in terms which closely resembled those used by the Gestalt psychologists. Physicists among us will not have had serious difficulties in following what I said in my second lecture—which was concerned with some basic concepts in natural science. But such discussions may appear too abstract to nonscientists. Actually, I was trying to prepare my audience for what I have to say in the first part of this lecture. For this purpose, I mentioned the general properties which any brain processes related to structured human perception are bound to have. But I have not yet said what specific physical processes (with such properties) I assume actually occur in the brain when we perceive one situation or another.

Speculations about the nature of these processes began fairly early in Gestalt psychology, in 1920.[1] It soon occurred to me that these processes might be electric currents which spread in the brain tissue as a continuous or volume conductor. But at that time I was working in Africa and had no access to some important new information about the anatomy of the brain. In a book published eighteen years later, I considered the same problem again and came to the same conclusion.[2] But this was still speculation, and only when a whole class of new psychological facts was thoroughly investigated could our question be answered in more specific terms and, therefore, with much more confidence.

The new facts are now called "figural after-effects." Early in the 1930's, Gibson discovered that when we look for some time at a curve which, geometrically, is part of a fairly large circle, this curve gradually becomes flatter, in other words, approaches the appearance of a straight line. When, afterwards, an objectively straight line is inspected which passes through the middle of the previously seen curve, this physically straight line now looks curved in the direc-

[1] W. Köhler. *Die physischen Gestalten in Ruhe und im stationären Zustand.* Braunschweig: Friedr. Vieweg & Sohn, 1920.
[2] W. Köhler. *The Place of Value in a World of Facts.* New York: Liveright Publishing Corp., 1938.

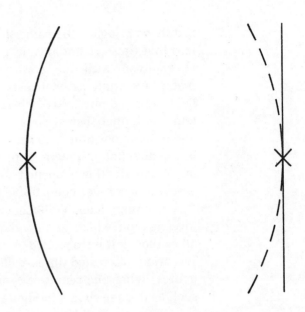

tion opposite to the one of that first curve (Figure 9). Gibson then tried a few other patterns and again found that under conditions of prolonged observation these patterns tended to "straighten out" just as that curve had done. It was later discovered that similar observations had occasionally been made by others. But, while these other investigators had regarded the observed changes as mere curiosities, Gibson recognized that they might be important facts and did some valuable experiments in the field. He was also bold enough to make such observations in another modality, namely kinesthesis, a person's perception of his own movements, and

Figure 9

results were again the same. It will be realized that Gibson's findings have one property in common with the earlier observations made by Gestalt psychologists and—in their field—by some physicists: when physical systems or human perceptions are given time and other opportunities to do so, they change in the direction of greater simplicity or regularity. Clearly, this happened also in Gibson's observations under comparable conditions.

A few years later, Wallach and I began an investigation which at first did not look at all as though it were related to Gibson's work. We were interested in so-called reversible figures. When the center of a simple pattern such as the one shown in Figure 10 is fixated

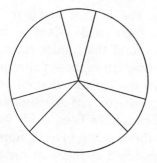

for some time, the part of the pattern which is first perceived as the "figure" (in Rubin's sense), namely the three narrow angles, suddenly disappears, and another part, consisting of the three larger angles, becomes the figure. After a short while, the first figure replaces the other again, and so forth. It seemed to us quite possible that, in either position, the cortical process corresponding to the figure seen at the time raises a local obstruction to its own continuation, and so weakens itself until, as a consequence, this process suddenly moves from its original location into the other possible area, and so forth.

This hypothesis had a far more general meaning than was at first realized.

If the process in question weakened itself (or blocked its own way) in a pattern in which another distribution of this process was possible, the result was a "reversal." But there was no reason why the first part of this sequence, the self-weakening of the process, should occur *only* in patterns which permitted the process to shift into another part of the pattern. Hence, we had to conclude that the process underlying any visual object would cause a local obstruction in its medium, and thereby cause a change in its own distribution—even when the change could not be a sudden reversal, a transfer to an entirely different location. Wallach and I tested this conclusion in experiments with a great number of visual patterns of all kinds. After a while it became obvious not only that any visual pattern or object is gradually altered when inspected for some time, but also that the change follows certain definite rules.

Moreover, we discovered that often, quite apart from the changes of the inspected object itself, other objects later shown in the same place or in its neighborhood were also affected. The most frequently observed effect of this kind was a displacement of such other objects, a displacement away from the area in which the originally inspected object had been located and, more specifically, away from the boundary of that first object.

Figure 11 shows an inspection pattern, Figure 12 a test pattern of a typical experiment. Figure 11—the pattern which is supposed to cause the obstruction—is fixated for some time and then replaced by Figure 12. If the prolonged inspection of the one object on the left side of the fixation point in Figure 11 causes an obstruction, then the two squares of the test pattern on the same side ought now to appear farther apart from each other than the squares on the other side. For the squares on the left side ought to have receded from the area between them, where the one rectangle was previously seen for some time—one square being displaced upward and the other downward. On the other side of the test figure, the squares ought also to have receded—one from the top rectangle of the (previously seen) inspection figure, the other from the lower rectangle, so that these squares are now seen nearer to each other. What is usually seen is a combination of

Figure 11

Figure 12

these two effects. These phenomena are very striking for some people, less for others.

When we had made a great many observations in this field, and therefore knew how figural after-effects behave, it became quite obvious that Gibson's experiments were special instances of the same general class, figural after-effects. Figural after-effects have since been investigated by many psychologists not only in the United States but also in other countries, particularly in Japan. Results have on the whole agreed well with our own findings. In one respect, our colleagues in Japan found that statements made by Wallach and me were too conservative. We had found that the time during which the first object must be shown if there is to be an obstruction effect need not be long. Our friends in Japan discovered that even a small fraction of a second is often sufficient at least for a short-lived effect. This is a most important discovery. For it shows that even when we look at an object only for a moment in ordinary life, this object may already be affected by the obstruction.

Wallach and I naturally assumed that the process which causes the obstruction is the cortical process of the visual object in question. Consequently, the rules which govern the figural after-effects in vision would also be the rules which characterize the physiological events underlying ordinary object perception.

These are the rules:

1. The cortical process must be such that its occurrence in the brain almost immediately begins to cause an obstruction in the tissue through which it passes.

2. The process must be stronger at or near the boundary of the object than far in its interior, because test objects shown inside the boundary recede from this boundary into the interior of the first object.

3. The process cannot be limited to the cortical area corresponding to the visual object itself, because often objects shown at a considerable distance from the first object still recede from it.

These rules suffice for identifying the process in terms of physics. At the present time, we know enough about the brain to extract from this knowledge a list of the processes which can possibly occur there.

The list is not very long. When it is completed, we compare its items and their functional properties with the rules which I just formulated. The result is simple. One item after another must be eliminated because it does not fit one rule or another. Eventually, only one item is left; but this item satisfies all conditions which follow from the rules. Electric currents which originate and spread in the brain tissue as a continuous or volume conductor are left as the only, and also the most satisfying, possibility.

How could such currents originate? For the sake of brevity, I will mention only the simplest case, that of an object the color of which differs from the color of the environment. The colors may, for instance, be two different degrees of brightness. I will surprise few physiologists if I say that in this situation a direct or quasi-steady current will begin to flow which passes through the object area and the environment area—more or less at right angles to the visual cortex, in one direction within the object area, in the opposite direction in its environment; these two parts of the flow are complemented by the flow which, on one side and the other of the active area, turns around the boundary of object and environment. At the active level, the current, flowing in opposite directions inside and outside the boundary, produces a most radical separation of the object from its environment, which makes the boundary a *functional* boundary. The behavior of the current thus explains the segregation of the visual object from its background—one of the facts which we could not understand during my first lecture.

I now return to the rules derived from the examination of figural after-effects. According to the *first* rule, the process related to a visual object must be able to cause an obstruction in the cortical medium. Will a cortical current cause such an obstruction? Undoubtedly, it will. For about a hundred years, physiologists have known that, when an electric current passes through cell surfaces in the nervous system, it immediately establishes an obstruction where it enters the cells. Naturally, the obstruction is stronger where the current is strong than it is in places where the flow is weak. The obstruction has two components, one physical in the usual sense of the word, the other a biological reaction of the cell to the entering current. We have no time for details, but I must mention that the biological component of the obstruction often survives the duration of the flow for long periods. In neurophysiological discussions, the obstruction goes under the name "electrotonus" (a term once used by Faraday with a somewhat different meaning). Anybody familiar with elementary physics realizes, of course, that the obstruction established by the current will force this current to change its distribution in the tissue; it will be weakened where the obstruction is particularly strong, and will flow with relatively increased intensity through regions where a weaker obstruction has been established. Since part of the obstruction persists when the original current has disappeared, the obstruction will still affect the flow of object currents when the original object is no longer present, but other objects appear in about the same region.

This is the main part of our explanation of figural after-effects. I should like to tell you what happened when I once had an opportunity to show several figural after-effects to a great neurophysiologist, Adrian in England. Adrian had never seen figural after-effects before, and I had not told him how we explained these phenomena. He made one observation after another; these agreed with the reports of other observers. After the fourth or fifth demonstration, he turned to me and said with a smile, "Nice demonstrations of electrotonus, aren't they, Köhler?" It was a pleasure to see that, after a few observations, a great scientist explained these phenomena precisely as we had done.

The object current, I said, causes the greatest obstruction or electrotonus where its own intensity is highest. Where will the current be strongest? This question brings us to the *second* rule which the object process must

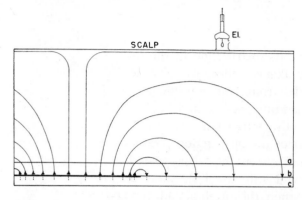

Figure 13. From W. Köhler, R. Held, and D. N. O'Connell, An investigation of cortical currents, *Proceedings of the American Philosophical Society* 96 (1952): 310.

obey. In Figure 13 the direction of the current which flows from an object area in the brain to the environment area is schematically represented, in the manner customary in physics. The current is represented by so-called lines of flow, the direction of which indicates the direction of the current in the various parts of the medium, while the density of the lines shows everywhere the local intensity of the flow. This intensity depends, of course, on the length of the loops along which the current must flow as it extends from a point in the object area to a point in the environment area and then returns to the former point. For this length measures the corresponding resistance. Only a little more than one-half of the loops is represented in this figure. It can easily be imagined how a loop will be completed below the horizontal line of Figure 13. Obviously, the loops near the boundary are shorter than the loops which begin further inside the object area. Consequently, the electric flow is more dense along the shorter loops—as indicated in the figure by the shorter distances between the lines of flow near the boundary. The same is true in the environment: here, too, the distance between the lines of flow is shortest near the boundary. Inside and outside, therefore, the most intense current flows near the boundary. It follows that our second rule or condition for the cortical process is fulfilled if this process is a current that connects the object area with the environment area.

I hardly need add that a cortical current also fits the *third* condition—that the cortical process must extend beyond the area of the cortical object. The very origin and nature of the currents which we are considering make it necessary that they pass through parts of the environment as well as through the object area.

When we had reached these conclusions, our further investigations could take two different directions. We could either try to discover whether the properties of cortical currents would also explain such perceptual facts as apparent movement, some geometrical illusions, gamma movement, and so forth; or we could try to decide more directly whether organized vision is actually accompanied by such currents. The former possibility would have meant a great deal of very hard work—which we were not yet ready to undertake because we could not yet be quite sure that such currents really existed. It was therefore decided to try first of all to prove the existence of cortical currents in direct physiological tests. To our knowledge, nobody had previously demonstrated their existence. And we realized that this would by no means be an easy task.

For instance with human subjects currents cannot, of course, be registered from the brain itself. Hence, one can only hope that at least a weak part of the cortical current passes through the skull and the scalp and can therefore be registered from the surface of the intact head. Other difficulties are related to the instruments to be used, for example, the amplifier needed for increasing the size of the necessarily weak potential differences at the surface of the head so as to obtain an outside current of an intensity sufficient to be recorded by the registering apparatus. There were also unexpected difficulties which we only gradually discovered and which we had to overcome one after another. Our first attempts were made at Princeton, I believe in 1947. Results were only mildly encouraging, because at the time we were only slowly becoming acquainted with some of the obstacles we had to overcome. The first clearly satisfactory tests were done at Swarthmore College, where I had the invaluable help of Richard Held, then my assistant.

A word about the places on the head where the electrodes were located. The visual cortex may be regarded as a rough copy of the retina of the eye. The fovea, the center of the visual field and the place of best vision, is cortically represented in the back of the head, right under the skull. The retinal places on the left and right sides of the fovea have their cortical counterparts in the interior of the brain; the more peripheral the retinal areas considered, the farther away from the cortical fovea and the deeper in the head are their cortical representations located. One electrode (which the physiologists call the active electrode) was placed on the skull where the cortical fovea lies, the other electrode was placed farther in front on a point quite distant from the visual cortex.

We soon discovered that it is far easier to obtain clear results when the object seen by the subject is slowly moving than when it is at rest. It will be seen immediately why this is the case. Our ignorance as to other important conditions was revealed to us when we once used visual conditions which we expected to *prevent* any positive results. Richard Held was the experimenter on this day, and I was the subject. A vertical line moved slowly, four times in succession, through my visual field while I fixated a faint mark in the middle of the field. I could not see or hear what the registering pen wrote on the recording paper. After a first sequence of four exposures, Held asked me whether we might try the same sequence of exposures again. I agreed. After the next sequence, Held whistled faintly. We did three or four experiments under the same conditions, and then Held suddenly asked me whether he might show me something. He tore a part of the recording paper from its support, came over to my place and showed me the registered curves. There were clear responses to all the exposures of the visual object. Figure 14 is an example of such a record, and Figure 15 another.

Now, because up to this point we had (for certain practical and statistical reasons) always given four or five successive exposures in one experiment, it had been necessary to move the recording paper very slowly. The time it took to give four exposures in a row amounted to half a minute. What happened during this period had therefore to be crowded into a very short space on the paper. As a result, the registered cortical reaction to one exposure was also temporally crowded so as to look quite short. But the reactions were not short from the point of view of the neurophysiologist. The registered responses shown in Figures 14 and 15 have a length of between 3 and 6 seconds, which, neurologically, is a very long time. Naturally, details of the responses could be more clearly seen, and the

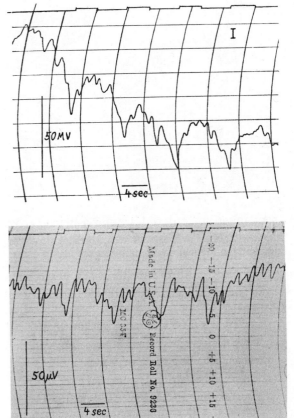

Figure 14. Note: The excursion downward in this and subsequent curves (Figures 14-19) does not indicate the direction of the current in the brain but, rather, a surface-positive polarity. This is only an effect of the special position of the active electrode. When this electrode is given other positions (or when it is placed on the brain itself), cortical currents always show a surface-negative polarity. From *Science* 110 (October 21, 1949): 415.

Figure 15. From *Proceedings of the American Philosophical Society* 96 (1952): 306.

responses could not give the impression of being short waves, if only one response was registered on a more adequately moving recording paper. How must the response look under such improved conditions? When the visual object appears in the periphery of the retina and the visual field, the cortical cur-

111

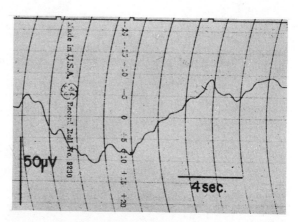

50μV

4sec.

Figure 16. From *Proceedings of the American Philosophical Society* 96 (1952): 298.

rent must be centered around a place far removed from the cortical fovea and, therefore, from the active electrode. Hence the registered current must first be weak. But when, now, the object gradually moves on the retina toward the fovea, its cortical representation moves in the brain toward the cortical fovea and the active electrode. Thus, the registered current must now grow, and must reach maximal size when it passes the cortical fovea and the electrode. Afterwards, this development will, of course, be reversed, because now the object moves away from the electrode as it gradually approaches the other periphery of the visual field. This may be seen in two illustrations. Figures 16 and 17 show that what I just predicted is exactly what happened.

The psychological facts which made it highly probable that the cortical process re-

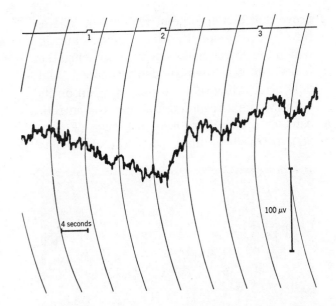

lated to visual objects is a steady current were the figural after-effects. These effects showed that such processes establish an obstruction within (and in the environment of) the area of the objects. It was therefore our next task to discover whether the currents registered from the visual cortex actually do establish such obstructions. That this is the case became quite probable when we found that slowly moving objects produced more conspicuous currents than did objects shown at rest. For, when the objects moved, they had, at each position in the brain, less time to establish a strong obstruction and thus to weaken themselves. Naturally, we wanted to

Figure 17. From *Cerebral Mechanisms in Behavior.* Permission of John Wiley and Sons, Inc.

prove that this argument was correct. There-fore we occasionally did experiments in which the object again slowly approached the fovea but was then suddenly stopped, and only after a few seconds started again on its path. My next record shows how the current behaves under these circumstances (Figure 18). In the beginning, when the object has

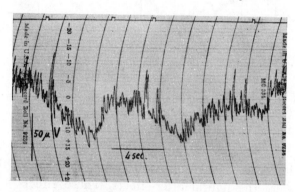

Figure 18. From *Proceedings of the American Philosophical Society* 96 (1952): 316.

just appeared in the periphery, there is the usual deflection downward as the object moves toward the fovea. But, this development is interrupted at the moment when the movement is interrupted, and the size of the current immediately begins to decrease until its intensity becomes steady at a much lower level during the interruption of the movement. When the movement is resumed, the flow increases again, until, as the object now begins to move toward the other periphery, its current once more declines, as it must. Such experiments were done repeatedly and

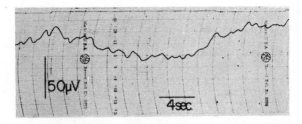

Figure 19. From
*Proceedings of the
American Philosophical
Society* 96 (1952):
319.

always showed the same effect of the transition from movement to rest of the object. This is the electrotonic effect.

It is therefore not astonishing that all records taken with the object at rest during the whole exposure show weaker responses than those taken when the object moves. Figure 19 is an example. In this case, the object (shown in the foveal region) did not move at all while the record was taken. Therefore, the angular shape of the curves seen in earlier figures has now disappeared, and what is left is a simple weak excursion, the size of which varies little.

For the sake of comparison, two records are shown of currents in the *auditory* cortex of human subjects, caused by noises. In Figure 20 the noise is a whistle produced by

Figure 20. From Record
12, W. Köhler and J.
Wegener, *Journal of
Cellular and Compara-
tive Physiology* 45
(1955) Suppl. 1: 35.

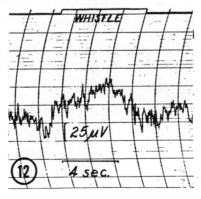

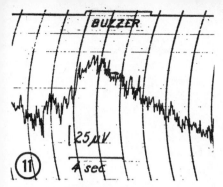

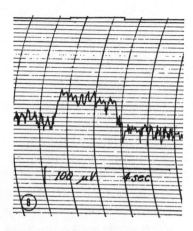

Figure 21. From Record
11, W. Köhler and
J. Wegener, *Journal
of Cellular and
Comparative
Physiology* 45
(1955) Suppl. 1: 35.

Figure 22. From Record
8, W. Köhler and
D. N. O'Connell,
*Journal of Cellular
and Comparative
Physiology* 49
(1957) Suppl. 2: 8.

the experimenter; in Figure 21, it is the sharp noise of a buzzer. It can be seen that these records from the auditory cortex exhibit the true, negative, polarity of cortical currents.

When the subjects were cats, we could simply put the electrodes on the brain of the animals. Under these circumstances, the registered responses were for the most part con-

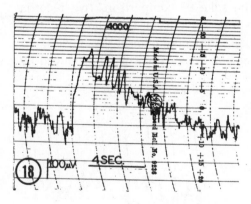

Figure 23. From Record
18, W. Köhler, W. D.
Neff, and J. Wegener,
*Journal of Cellular
and Comparative
Physiology* 45
(1955) Suppl. 1: 13.

116

siderably stronger—as was to be expected. Figure 22 shows the brain current of a cat when a bright rectangle appeared before its eyes. And in Figure 23 we have the auditory current of a cat when a strong tone of a frequency of 4,000 cycles per second was used as the stimulus. The tone seems to cause a strong electrotonic obstruction, for the intensity of the current decreases while the tone is still heard.

Are these currents really related to facts of perception? Most probably they are. For when we tried to take such records from the brains of cats who were under the influence of a strong anesthetic, or deeply asleep as an after-effect of the anesthesia, we never obtained records of cortical currents. Several times, when the cat was merely asleep and no currents appeared in the records, we just squeezed the animal's ear a little, and a few seconds later the same perceptual stimulation, which before had no effect, now produced a perfectly clear response. An experimenter is delighted by such observations.

Enough of cortical currents. The demonstration of their actual existence is a good step forward in our exploration of the relation between psychological facts and underlying brain processes. It is also important to know that the obstructions observed in figural after-effects can now safely be regarded as electrotonic effects produced by such cortical currents. Moreover, we now know also that, as currents flowing in a volume conductor, these processes follow the principle once formulated by Maxwell and Planck: the currents have to be considered as functional wholes. For when currents spread in a continuous medium, the local flow always depends on the distribution of the current as a whole.

Unfortunately, we cannot yet give such perceptual observations as apparent movement or optical illusions a clear interpretation in terms of brain currents. This is not possible for simple technical reasons. In order to proceed in such directions, one would have to obtain records of the whole distribution of the cortical currents within the brain, of interactions between several such currents, and so forth. With present techniques one cannot take such records. Naturally, one electrode attached to the head or the brain over part of the active region does not give us information on how the given brain currents behave in the tissue as a whole. To be sure, there is one property of, say, the visual currents about which no doubt is left. It will be remembered that, when a visual object first appears in the periphery of the visual field, a weak current immediately appears in the records when the active electrode has been placed over the cortical fovea —although at the time a great distance separates the location of the cortical object, the source of the current, from this electrode. It is therefore no longer astonishing that visual perception often demonstrates interaction across considerable visual distances. The currents do spread widely.

That stimulation establishes steady currents in other parts of the nervous system has repeatedly been shown by Adrian[3] and by Barron and Matthews[4] in England. But these investigators did not take records of *brain* currents. In this country, when we had just done our first recordings of visual currents from the heads of human beings, Goldring and O'Leary actually obtained currents from the brains of rabbits under conditions of peripheral stimulation.[5, 6] Not being psychologists, however, they did not know how well their results fitted many facts in perception, and they therefore decided that their findings could hardly be related to perception at all. Perception was then—and still is —widely believed to be a matter of strictly lo-

[3] E. D. Adrian. General principles of nervous activity, *Brain* 70 (1947): 1-17

[4] D. H. Barron and B. H. C. Matthews. The interpretation of potential changes in the spinal cord, *J. Physiol.* 92 (1938): 276-321.

[5] S. Goldring and J. L. O'Leary. Experimentally derived correlates between EEG and steady cortical potential, *J. Neurophysiol.* 14 (1951): 275-288.

[6] S. Goldring and J. L. O'Leary. Summation of certain enduring sequelae of cortical activation in the rabbit, *EEG Clin. Neurophysiol.* 3 (1951): 329-340.

cal processes. What, under the circumstances, could freely spreading currents have to do with perception? The old belief in the primary importance of purely local facts is still very much alive. In fact, it is now strengthened by the invention of new devices, the micro-electrodes, which permit the psychologist to take records from individual cells in the nervous system. One cannot object to the use of such tools. Some questions concerning the elements of the nervous system are now being answered with their help. But they contribute little to our knowledge of molar, macroscopic brain processes, which is far more important for our understanding of psychological facts. Maxwell and Planck, it seems, have simply spoken in vain.

But may the Gestalt psychologist not be accused of being a bit narrow-minded himself? So far, I have spoken only of perception and of related brain processes. Are the Gestalt psychologists not interested in other parts of their science? They are, and have been, for some time. For they have also investigated problems in memory, in recall, in thinking, and also in the field of motivation. About thinking I am going to speak in the next lecture. Motivation (which was Kurt Lewin's main interest) I will not discuss because we do not yet know how Lewin's important work is related to Gestalt psychology, the theme of my lectures. But our investigations in the field of memory we will consider now. It will soon be seen that they are closely related to what I have said so far.

The term "memory" is often used in a very general sense. We will distinguish between *learning*, a process which establishes traces in the nervous system, and these traces themselves, which form the basis for memory in a narrower sense. And both have to be distinguished from such facts as actual *remembering*, which may mean either recalling or recognizing, both obviously being effects of traces on present psychological processes. When we first began to be interested in this group of facts, all questions referring to it seemed to differ from the problems with which we had become acquainted when studying perception. In this respect, we soon discovered, we were mistaken. For some of the problems in the new field proved to be closely related to concepts with which the study of perception had made us familiar. Take the form of remembering which is called *recognition*. An object appears before us in present perception and is immediately seen as being like this or that earlier experience. This is an extremely frequent event, and it is so familiar that one seldom asks questions about it. But as soon as we began to ask such questions, we discovered that at least in one respect we were again confronted with an example of those *interactions* with which we had to deal when we studied perception. What does recognition mean? It means that a present fact, usually a perceptual one, makes contact with a corresponding fact in memory, a trace, a contact which gives the present perception the character of being known or familiar. But memory contains a tremendous number of traces, all of them representations of earlier experiences which must have been established by the processes accompanying such earlier experiences. Now, why does the present perceptual experience make contact with the trace of the *right* earlier experience? This is an astonishing achievement. Nobody seems to doubt that the *selection* is brought about by the similarity of the present experience and the experience of the corresponding earlier fact. But since this earlier experience is not present at the time, we have to assume that the trace of the earlier experience resembles the present experience, and that it is the similarity of our present experience (or the corresponding cortical process) and that trace which makes the selection possible. This explanation of recognition leads to a radical consequence, a consequence which establishes a close relation between the fact of recognition and the physiological facts discussed up to now. Experiments have shown that correct visual recognition may occur when the original experience was located in one part of the visual field and cortex, and the new experience is located in a different part, often a part far removed from the place of the original experience and its trace. Consequently, we are now confronted with a new example of interaction, a rapid interaction across very large distances in the brain. This seems to mean that a process directly related to the present visual experience, its cortical current, spreads far from its source into a distant region, the region of the trace. It does seem that recognition is a field effect, the same kind that had to be postulated in some instances of perceptual interaction. Perhaps this is no longer a surprising conclusion, for we have seen that cortical currents registered from human heads do spread far around their sources.

Our earliest psychological experiments in the field of memory referred to a somewhat different fact. My assistant, von Restorff, and I considered the following problem. When subjects learn a series of items, the effect of this learning is disturbed if, between the learning and the test of recall, the subjects have to deal with items of a similar kind. Does such a similarity disturb learning also when the various items *in* the series to be learned resemble one another? We investigated this problem in several groups of experiments. In one such group, the subjects were shown three series of items, the three series being separated by intervals of several days.

All three series contained eight pairs of items. The items of each pair were shown simultaneously. Six pairs of the series were all of one kind, a seventh pair was of a second, and the eighth pair of a third kind. In the *first* series, the six similar pairs were made up of nonsense syllables; one pair consisted of nonsense figures; and the remaining pair of two-digit numbers. In the *second* series, six pairs of numbers were combined with one pair of syllables and one pair of figures; the *third* series contained six pairs of nonsense figures, one pair of syllables, and one pair of numbers. In the three series taken together, the three classes of items were thus given the same chance of being learned and afterwards recalled, either as individual pairs or as pairs in an accumulation of six pairs. Table 1[7] contains the results of the tests. For all three kinds of items, the differences between the crowded (or homogeneous) and the isolated pairs are so great that no statistical tests are needed to prove that the differences are reliable. "Association," as psychologists call the tested connection within the pairs, is clearly superior for the isolated pairs. The same result was generally obtained by other psychologists who later did experiments of this kind.

[7] From H. von Restorff. Über die Wirkung von Bereichsbildungen im Spurenfeld, *Psychologische Forschung* 18 (1933): 299-342. (Table 4, page 305.)

TABLE 1

Recall of Crowded and Isolated Items

Syllables		Figures		Numbers		Total	
C	I	C	I	C	I	C	I
13	41	8.7	43	15	41	36.7	125
27%	85%	18%	90%	31%	85%	25%	87%

C = crowded; I = isolated.

What does this mean? It will be remembered that when a number of objects are shown simultaneously in visual perception, all these objects may appear as members of one large group—or they may be seen as members of two or more separate sub-groups. Distances between the objects and greater or lesser similarities of the objects decide whether one large or several small—or one large and a few smaller—groups are formed. If, in a given case, distance plays no rôle in deciding what groups are formed, it will be similarity of the items which determines the formation of larger or smaller groups. Consequently, if we were to show together six pairs of objects of one kind, a single pair of a different kind, and a further single pair of a third kind, the total number of pairs would be seen as articulated in this fashion: there would be a large unitary group of six pairs of one class and two smaller groups each containing just one pair. Obviously, the larger and the two small groups would each be functionally united, but separated from one another. Hence, the pairs in the larger group would lose their independence, while the two small groups which contain only one pair each would not be affected either by the homogeneous large group or by each other.

Now, is grouping of this kind established only when the object-pairs in question are simultaneously presented? Or is the same articulation also present when, other things being equal, the object-pairs are shown in succession? Very simple observations demonstrate that when such pairs (with their similarities and dissimilarities) are successively presented, the total sequence still tends to be organized and articulated; thus one large group of pairs of one kind and two small groups of one pair each (of a second and third kind) are again formed. Interaction within the large group would again be strong, and the pairs of this group would therefore become united or lose their independence, but this influence would not extend to the two small segregated pairs, which would also not strongly influence each other.

Suppose that specific recall within a pair is easier when this pair remains independent than when the pair becomes a member of a large group of pairs whose similarity causes individual members to lose their distinguishing characteristics to a considerable extent. Then results of our experiment could be interpreted as being caused by organization and articulation within the sequence, the series as a whole.

126

We did take this hypothetical step from organization in simultaneous perception to organization and articulation of successively presented pairs as an explanation of the findings shown in Table 1.

This procedure greatly disturbed some psychologists who did not like the fact that such concepts as organization and articulation were now creeping even into the field of learning and memory. One psychologist did experiments which were meant to test our results, but his experimental conditions were quite different from those used in our investigation.[8] *Nothing worked*; but I am not surprised by his negative result, because his own observations clearly showed that in his different experimental series and under his conditions, articulation or isolation in the perceptual sense simply could not occur.

Even so, our friendly opponent said, the results which von Restorff and Köhler have obtained have nothing to do with such Gestalt concepts as organization and articulation. For they can easily be explained in simpler terms with which every psychologist is familiar: in series of items which subjects have to learn there is always a strong tendency for all individual items (or pairs) to disturb the learning of the other items in the series—by competing individual recall tendencies which

[8] L. Postman and L. W. Phillips. Studies in incidental learning: I. The effects of crowding and isolation, *Journal of Experimental Psychology* 48 (1954): 48-56.

extend through the whole series. This disturbing tendency is greater when the items resemble each other than when the items are dissimilar. Consequently, the so-called isolated items or pairs, resembling less the other items or pairs of Köhler's series, are less disturbed by such wrong recall tendencies. Thus one can explain the isolation effect in simple terms and need not refer to such mysteries as organization and articulation at all.

But not always are the most simple relations in our thinking at the same time the relations which best fit the nature of the investigated material. I continued the investigation of the isolation effect with a different procedure. I will not try to describe these new experiments, some of which were completed only recently. The main point is this: one can construct experimental series in such a way that, according to the opposing explanation of the isolation effect, one has to expect one result, and from the point of view of organization and articulation, precisely the opposite result. Actual results were perfectly clear and statistically significant: it is articulation in the organizational sense, not the number and size of individual similarities in the series, on which the isolation effect depends.[9]

[9] *Editors' note*: This statement refers to experiments which Professor Köhler conducted but had not yet prepared for publication.

Why spend so much time on a very special problem in the psychology of learning, the isolation effect? My answer is this: From a theoretical point of view this is surely not a very special problem. For when thinking about it more thoroughly, one discovers that this is a matter of general principle. The main question is this: Do concepts derived from studies of perception really apply to problems in the field of memory? If in the case of the isolation effect, the answer is a clear *yes*, one can hardly stop at this point for the following reason. I have just pointed out that when an individual pair of items is segregated or isolated, it becomes independent of masses of other items in the series. In this case, we have seen, effective association and corresponding recall within this pair are not disturbed by absorption of the pair in the series as a whole. But what about the nature of the association within the isolated pair itself? Surely, the items of the pair itself interact. What else does the term "association" mean? It is this interaction within the pair, the association, which is not disturbed when the pair is isolated. This kind of interaction within the pair, the association, we may call a *positive* effect. Is it necessarily different from the kind of interaction which the isolation *prevents*, the interaction of remote pairs or items with the crucial pair? Interaction with such outside items would be harmful, a *negative* influence. But if the same kind of interaction occurred, undisturbed, between the two items of the crucial pair, would its effect then also be harmful? What do I mean by the expression "kind of interaction"? The answer is simple. The detrimental interaction (which is prevented by isolation) is obviously a matter of the similarities between the items or pairs involved. Is the same true of the "approved" interaction within the pair which we call an association? It would be a parsimonious hypothesis if we assumed that the positive and the negative influences are basically of the same nature—with the consequence that association of the two items in the pair should also be strengthened when these two items resemble each other.

If this were true, the central concept in the field of memory, the concept of association, would become most closely related to elementary facts in perception. Suppose we look at a simple pair of objects in the visual field. We remember that formation of the *pair* as a unified perceptual group is facilitated if the two objects are similar. Hence, if perceptual similarity of two objects helps to unite them as one pair, would not this unification in perception be accompanied by the formation of a correspondingly unified pair as a memory trace? If this unification were the same thing as what we usually call an association, it would, of course, follow that similarity of two items which are to be associated must facilitate their actual association.

The present tentative interpretation of the concept of association will appear quite plausible if we add the following consideration. An association is often said to be a matter of contiguity, which means neighborhood of two items in space or time or both. We know that this condition, a short distance between objects, favors their unification in perception. If this condition of perceptual organization, close neighborhood, favors the formation of a perceptual pair, then the preservation of this unification in the realm of corresponding memory traces would provide an explanation of the traditional "association by contiguity." Now, is there any reason why only one condition which facilitates perceptual unification should thus become effective in an association? What about similarity of the objects in question? Clearly, if the effect of neighborhood or contiguity in perceptual pairing is afterwards represented in memory, the effect of other conditions which favor perceptual unification is likely also to be preserved in memory—with the result that they, too, would favor "association" and corresponding recall. This would be true of similarity of the items in question—and of any further condition which favors pair-formation in perception.

For the moment we are particularly interested in the rôle which similarity plays in perceptual unification. If it could be shown that associations of two similar items are more easily established, that is, give better recall, than associations of dissimilar items, then our assumption that association is an after-effect of pair-formation in original experience, say in perception, would be greatly strengthened. We once tried to decide in simple experiments whether presentation of similar objects produces more effective associations than presentation of dissimilar items. Results were clearly positive. It does seem to be true that principles of perceptual organization are, without any essential modification, valid in memory, too. Postman does not like the fact that, in this fashion, the old association by mere contiguity is threatened by the intrusion of Gestalt thinking, and he argues strongly against the intrusion and against our experiments.[10] The experiments, I will candidly say, are perhaps not yet entirely conclusive. But I am grateful to Postman; his arguments tell me exactly what further tests must now be done in order to reach a clear decision.[11] At times, work in psychology does become a lively affair.

[10] L. Postman and D. A. Riley. A critique of Köhler's theory of association, *Psychological Review* 64 (1957): 61-72.

[11] *Editors' note*: These experiments were still in the planning stage at the time of Professor Köhler's death.

IV · WHAT IS THINKING?

What do we mean by thinking? Common language is not particularly careful in its use of psychological terms. Take the word "thinking" itself. What does it really mean? Sometimes, it means that a person is merely considering certain situations or events of his past. "What are you thinking about?" we may ask a friend who, at the moment, looks a bit absent-minded. And the friend answers, "Oh, I was just thinking of that lovely scenery near Amalfi in Italy, where I spent a few days last spring." Here, thinking clearly means no more than an inspection of memories. Again, somebody may ask us, "Now, did you write that letter?" And we answer, "Well, I thought I would do so after lunch; but then I became interested in something else." Here, thinking is practically a synonym for having an intention. In both cases, the thinking involved is no particular achievement. It just refers to having mental contents, in the absence of corresponding perceptual realities or actions.

But the same term is also used when thinking does become an achievement, that is, when it is productive. This happens when it changes our mental environment by solving problems which this environment offers. Now this is, of course, an entirely different story. The range of such achievements is tremendous. It extends from the solution of very simple problems in everyday life to veritable mental revolutions such as sometimes occur in the minds of great scientists and may then affect the lives of human beings forever afterward. It is with thinking in this sense, with productive thinking, that I will now deal. In doing so, I will proceed as follows. I will give several concrete examples— all extremely simple, but at the same time representative of what always seems to happen when we solve problems. I hope my examples will not be too simple.

A first point: when dealing with a problem, we are invariably occupied with a certain material, with a given situation which contains this problem. The situation in question may be given in ordinary perception, or in the form of a mathematical expression before us, or in what might be called a purely mental picture of certain facts. Something is to be achieved with regard to such a situation; but, as the situation is given, it cannot be achieved. How must we change the situation so that the difficulties disappear and our problem is solved?

A few remarks about what I have just called the "given material." What does "given" mean in this expression? In many cases, the "given" is not simply available to all persons. For, generally speaking, the material is such that only people who are acquainted with certain other facts, apart from the actually given, can fully appreciate the nature of this material and thus the problem which it offers. In other words, some previous learning is often needed not only for the solution of a problem but also for its understanding as a problem.

Take this example which is mentioned in an interesting book by Karl Duncker.[1] Around 1910, the medical profession became acquainted with a most important possibility in their field. Tumors in the human organism may be destroyed (or their growth inhibited) by exposing the new tissue to the radiation of a radioactive substance. So long as the tumor is located near the surface of the organism there is, of course, no particular problem. The beam of the radiation is carefully directed toward the affected part. But what about tumors located far below the surface, as they often are? If the physician now directs the beam of the radiation toward the tumor, the radiation will affect, and possibly destroy, first of all the healthy tissue between the surface and the tumor—which should not happen under any circumstance. This is the problem. And what is the solution? The doctor divides the radioactive material into a number of much smaller parts which emit

[1] K. Duncker. On problem-solving (trans. by Lynne S. Lees), *Psychological Monographs* 58 (1945). (Whole No. 270.)

correspondingly smaller amounts of the radiation. These smaller parts he distributes around the patient's body in such fashion that the openings of the containers from which the radiations issue all point at the tumor. If this is done properly, weak radiations, which can do little harm, will pass from several places through the patient's healthy tissue between the surface and the tumor; but where the weak radiations meet, that is, just at the place of the tumor, they will add up to a powerful radiation and may thus destroy the dangerous growth.

Now, quite apart from this solution of the problem—an example of productive thinking—what can we say about the so-called given situation in the present case and the problem which it offers? Only people who have a certain knowledge of physics and of anatomy will see this situation and the problem so clearly that they understand both and can therefore be expected to do something about them. Obviously, the man who first discovered the solution had the required knowledge. What I have called the given situation is, therefore, in the present case not merely a matter of present facts. It is just as much a matter of previous training, the results of which pervade those facts.

Here is another example from an entirely different field. Somebody tells us that all numbers of the form *abcabc* can be divided by 13. Our task is to show that this is invariably true. But there is a problem for this reason: the symbol *abcabc*—what has it to do with any particular number? Those who are not familiar with certain symbols used in mathematics will, of course, never be able to tell. And, in the present case, the symbolism is particularly elusive. The mere position in a series of digits must here be understood to mean certain classes of numbers, the first position on the right side the class of numbers from 0 to 9, the next position multiples of 10, and so forth. Moreover, the symbol *abcabc* indicates that the three digits on the left side are the same as the three digits on the right side. Even when we now hear that "any number of the form *abcabc*" may mean, for instance, 326,326 or 985,985 or any six-place number of which the first three digits and the last three are identical—even then we may not see at once what 13 has to do with them all. Clearly, we are not meant merely to try out all individual instances of the form *abcabc* (of which there are approximately 1,000); rather, we are expected to show why the very form of this symbol makes it necessary for any number which fits this form to be a multiple of 13. Once the answer is known, it will, of course, seem fairly obvious. Just the same, before the problem is solved, the individual may have serious difficulties; he may not even see how to approach the solution. Here is the answer: in the symbol *abcabc*, it will be remembered, the six positions of the digits *a*, *b*, and *c* have a numerical meaning. On the left side, *a* means so and so many times 100,000, *b* means so and so many times 10,000, and so forth. Consequently, the whole symbol is identical with *abc*,000 + *abc* or *abc*(1000 + 1), just as (in one of my examples) 326,326 is, of course, 326,000 + 326 or 326(1000 + 1) or 326 × 1001. Thus there is a concrete number after all, 1001, that is contained in all numbers of the form *abcabc*. Since this is a constant factor in all numbers *abcabc*, whatever *a* and *b* and *c* may be, this constant factor must be a multiple of 13, if it is really true that all numbers of the form *abcabc* can be divided by 13. It will be seen at once that 1001 is indeed 13 × 77; thus, numbers of the form *abcabc* can be divided not only by 13, the number mentioned in the problem, but also by 7 and by 11.

You will have realized that, indeed, only people familiar with the symbolism of algebra can be expected to solve such problems quickly. It generally does not help very much if, just when the problem is given, we add an explanation of what *abcabc* means in algebra. If people who are expected to solve the present problem must at the same time try to remember this fairly abstract definition, their psychological situation will become so complicated that they are not likely to find the solution. Those who are well trained in algebra are, of course, no longer in need of the definition; in such people, the meaning of a symbol such as *abcabc* has practically crept into the very perception of *abcabc*—an important form of memory which, many years ago, British psychologists called "assimilation."

"Assimilation" plays a tremendously important rôle in our mental processes. The term means that, when certain perceptual facts have over and over again been accompanied by *important* other facts, the characteristics of the latter are no longer remembered as separate data; rather, these characteristics have gradually filtered into the *perceptual* facts themselves—so that now these facts are imbued with such characteristics as their meanings. That is, for instance, true of the perceived red or green traffic lights at intersections. Fortunately, we no longer have to think about the definition of the symbol red when "red" as a circular percept appears before us at an intersection. Long ago, a red circle in such a place became imbued with the meaning "stop" or "closed," just as a green circle is now imbued with the meaning "open" or "go ahead." Obviously, this kind of thing greatly facilitates our behavior in many situations. In mathematics, the same psychological fact, assimilation, operates all the time. When we see this cross $+$ between numbers, it now tells us directly that this is a matter of addition; it now simply looks it—however arbitrary the choice of the symbol for the operation "adding" may once have been. In other words, the cross in such a situation has assimilated its meaning of addition.

Giving meaning to facts before us is not, of course, the only way in which memory, of one kind or another, is essential to productive thinking. Take the obvious fact that often the solving of a problem takes considerable time; that we have to take several steps in succession before the solution is completed. If we did not remember the earlier steps when the later steps are to be taken, how could we possibly choose the later steps correctly? In addition, sometimes the solution will not occur unless we add to the given situation certain other facts, not now present, which, when considered together with the given material, may make us see the right procedure immediately. It is only memory or its consequence, recall, that can deliver such helpful additional material just when it is needed.

But let us not go too far. Some psychologists have suggested that the solving of problems is *throughout* a matter of previous learning and of corresponding recall. I do not agree with this suggestion. To be sure, it will help a person to solve a problem if, say, one part or step of the solution is familiar to him. But this fact does not tell us what happened at the time when that part or step first occurred in an earlier period of the subject's life, and could thus become familiar. In other words, such a statement merely pushes all questions concerning productive thinking into the past; it does not answer them. We should also not forget that, often in the history of science, problems could only be solved by people who managed to overcome the influence of habitual conceptions, that is, of ways of thinking established by previous learning. Memory may be an obstacle as well as a help in this field.

Unfortunately, those who refer to previous learning as soon as they are confronted with novel, and therefore particularly interesting, psychological phenomena show little interest in these phenomena as such. In fact, vague references to previous learning have, first of all, the effect of pushing possibly important facts aside. This has also happened in the present case. As a result, some aspects of productive thinking are never mentioned by those to whom "previous learning" has become the answer to almost any psychological question. We will not make this mistake. Rather, we will now return to our analysis of the various processes actually involved in problem-solving.

There is one psychological fact that plays a central rôle in productive thinking. This fact is a subject's awareness of *relations*. Awareness of relations is a curious phenomenon. It will be remembered that many tend to approach psychological situations with a certain prejudice. Such situations, they often assume, consist originally of numerous, mutually independent, parts. These parts, they add, may become connected by such processes as association or conditioning. But, apart from such secondary connections, they say, the mental scene does consist of separate local facts; and when these separate facts have become connected and, as a consequence, now tend to appear together, it is a purely external attachment that has this effect. This is, of course, an entirely wrong picture of mental life. Some mental facts are quietly omitted from this picture. What is missing is, for instance, our awareness of relations. When seeing two parallel lines like those in Figure 24, we may be aware not only of these lines as two visual entities, but also of the fact that the one on the left side is longer than the one on the right side. This is awareness of a particular relation. Similarly, when of two surfaces before us one is gray and the other white, we may be aware of the surfaces not as mutually indifferent parts of the field, but as one being brighter than the

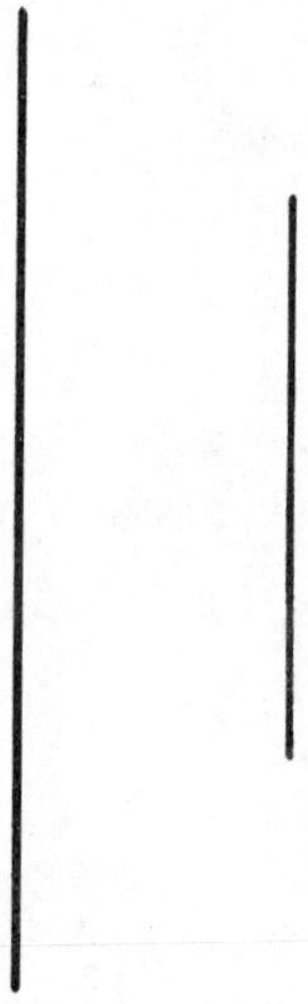

Figure 24

142

other, and so forth. I said, such relations *may* appear. In an average visual field, hundreds of relations may appear, once we begin to be interested in them and to single out pairs of data that exhibit the relations in question. Generally speaking, particular relations emerge only when our attention has the right direction for their appearance. But when we are aware of a relation, how does this fact compare with the thesis that, apart from secondary associations, mental situations consist of strictly separate parts? Can relations of which we become aware be called further independent parts or elements in this sense? Surely not. When, of the two lines in the figure, one is recognized as being longer than the other, this relation is not an independent third fact or piece at all. We are aware of this relation as depending upon the characteristics of the two lines, or as following from those characteristics. In other words, when we apprehend a relation, we have insight into its dependence upon the nature of the related data.

The next step we have to take is this: we have to recognize that probably all problems with which we may be confronted, and also the solutions of such problems, are matters of relations. So long as problems *are* problems, the materials in question exhibit *some* relations; but these special relations are such that a difficulty arises. However, we may now discover other relations in the material which make the difficulty disappear. In some instances, we are at first unable to see any relations in the material which are relevant to our task. When this happens, we have to inspect the given situation until, eventually, it does exhibit relations from which a solution can be derived. Consequently, not only does our understanding of the problem depend upon our awareness of certain relations; we can also not solve the problem without discovering certain new relations. For the most part, such relations are not quite as simple and directly accessible as are the relations of size or brightness in my examples. Often they are of a far more abstract or conceptual kind; and, almost always, we have to deal not with one relation but, rather, with whole sets of them, and thus with relations among relations.

Consider my first example of a problem and its solution. What was the problem? When trying to destroy a tumor in the interior of a patient's body, the medical people soon realized that, since the radiation is gradually weakened as it passes through a medium such as human tissue, the destructive effect of the radiation will be maximal at and near the healthy surface, not at the tumor, where it ought to be maximal. Clearly, the problem is a matter of geometrical relations and of physical relations which depend upon the former. And what was the essential part of the solution? It was a redistribution of the radiating material around the body, that is, a change in the geometrical relations so that, physically, the tissue at and near the surface was no longer harmed, while the effect at the place of the tumor remained about as strong as before. Thus, geometrical relations were changed in order to establish satisfactory physical relations.

In my second example, the one concerning numbers of the form *abcabc* and the particular number 13, the problem first seemed insoluble, because we could not discover *any* relation between the abstract symbol *abcabc* and the specific number 13. The solution consisted of the discovery that, after all, all numbers of the type *abcabc* are characterized by certain relations and that, as a consequence, they do contain a particular numerical factor, namely 1001, a fact which enabled us to establish a simple relation between the abstract symbol and the number 13.

One more simple example—just to show that the solution of problems seems always to be a matter of realizing certain new relations. Suppose we consider a situation in elementary geometry. There is a circle with

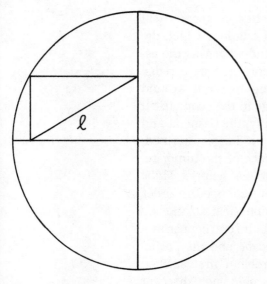

Figure 25 the radius r, and in this circle I construct a rectangle (Figure 25). The problem is the following. If I now draw the line l within the rectangle, what is the length of this line? Not everybody will be able to give the right answer immediately. And yet, the answer is extraordinarily simple. Just as in many other cases, we find the solution by adding something to the given material—in our particular case, by adding just one line. The given line l is a diagonal of the given rectangle. But rectangles have two diagonals. If we add the second, what do we find? The second diagonal extends from the center of the circle to its circumference and is, therefore, the radius. Now, since the two diagonals of a

146

rectangle are, for simple reasons of symmetry, always equally long, our line l must necessarily also have the length r, the length of the radius, whatever particular shape the rectangle may have. Once more, the solution of the problem is a matter of discovering a relation—to be sure, in this problem a relation discernible only after the second diagonal has been added to the given material. Once this has happened, we recognize, of course, why the addition of the second diagonal and the corresponding new relation bring about the solution. In other words, once the material has been properly changed, we understand perfectly why the addition of the second diagonal gives us the required answer. This is what we call *insight* in thinking.

Changes in given situations that bring forth the decisive relations are not always mere additions. Often, the decisive step is what we may call a restructuring of the given material. One more example from elementary mathematics, this one concerning what the mathematicians call infinite series. For example, the series of the integers is an infinite series. It can be continued without ever coming to an end. This applies also to a so-called geometrical series such as 1, 1/2, 1/4, 1/8, etc., where each successive item is derived from the preceding item by multiplying the latter by 1/2. Now, some such infinite series have the remarkable property that, however far the series may be extended, the sum of its members never grows beyond a certain limit. For instance, the sum of the items in the series $1 + 1/2 + 1/4$ . . . and so forth, never grows beyond the value 2, irrespective of how many further items we add. Let us now take a slightly more complicated series: $1 - 1/2 + 1/3 - 1/4 + 1/5$ . . . , etc., in which plus and minus signs are alternated as the series proceeds. Our problem is this. Does the sum of the items in *this* series remain finite, or does it grow indefinitely as the series continues? This series may be restructured without altering it by combining its items in pairs in the following manner:

$1 - (1/2 - 1/3) - (1/4 - 1/5) - (1/6 - 1/7) - $ . . . . It will be realized that this is still precisely the same series, only written in a different form. Now, the result of this operation is perfectly obvious. In each parenthesis, a smaller number is subtracted from a larger number; in the first parenthesis, for instance, $1/3$ from $1/2$; in the second parenthesis, $1/5$ from $1/4$, and so on. Consequently, all parentheses as such contain positive numbers, and all these positive numbers are to be subtracted from 1. We see at once that the result, however long the series may be, must be a number of smaller than 1. Is

this all we can say about it? By no means. I
now do another regrouping:

$$(1 - 1/2) + (1/3 - 1/4) + (1/5 - 1/6) +$$

.... In each parenthesis, the second number,
which is to be subtracted, is again smaller
than the first. Consequently, the contents of
all parentheses are positive numbers. And,
since these positive numbers are to be added
to the first, which is $1 - 1/2 = 1/2$, the sum
of all parentheses must give a number which
is larger than $1/2$. The sum of the items for
the whole series must therefore be greater
than $1/2$. This sum, we found before, can
never grow beyond 1, and now we have discovered that the sum cannot be smaller than
$1/2$. Consequently, the sum lies between $1/2$
and 1. How was the solution achieved? We
first grouped the items in one way, and found
one relation for the sum: Sum < 1. Then
we grouped the items in another way, and
found a second relation for the same sum:
Sum $> 1/2$.[2] Thus the sum is caught between
two limits. In more general terms, both regroupings have led to the discovery of es-

[2] *Editors' note*: The two regroupings are distinguished by this, that in the first, the final member
of the original series is the reciprocal of an odd
number, in the second, that of an even number. It
is easily seen that these considerations hold in just
the same way even if another member is added to
the original series. The sum is thus actually the
"same" sum.

sential relations, and thus we have obtained a result, the logical necessity of which we clearly understand.

It will be seen that I am using the terms insight and understanding as names for the same psychological fact. Now, these terms have not always been popular in psychology; for instance, the word insight has for years been printed in quotes, as though it referred to something funny or mysterious. In order to show that the terms insight and understanding correspond to perfectly obvious human experiences, I will now introduce a very simple situation in which clear understanding of certain relations, and therefore insight, is at first confronted with absence of understanding and insight in another respect.

In the following series, the first two lines are easily understood.

```
0   1   2   3    4    5    6    7    8 . . .
0   1   4   9   16   25   36   49   64 . . .
    1   3   5   7    9   11   13   15 . . . .
```

The first consists of part of the series of the integers and the second consists of their squares. What of the third line? Obviously, I subtracted each square from the next. But what about the results of my subtractions as a series? They are identical with the series of the odd numbers. And this may not have been understood immediately. Is it an accident that the series in the third line is that of the odd numbers? So long as we do not know, we can, of course, not predict whether, if our three lines were continued, further items in the third line would also be odd numbers. We cannot tell in the absence of insight into what has just happened. And so far, there is perhaps no such insight. It was easy to follow with insight everything down to the individual subtractions. But when the results of the successive subtractions, so far, became identical with the series of the odd numbers, some fail to understand. I hope that the contrast is quite clear and that, therefore, it is also clear that we do not refer to funny or mysterious notions when we use such words as "understanding" and "insight."

We do, of course, suspect that there is a good reason for the appearance of the odd numbers in the third line, but we cannot yet be sure. In actual fact, there is a good reason. For, in the second series, we have the sequence of the squares of the integers. Now, the integers themselves, in alternation, are odd and even numbers. When we square an odd number, squaring means, of course, that we multiply this odd number by itself, that is, by an odd number—which must yield an odd number. On the other hand, when we square an even number, squaring means that we multiply this even number by itself, that is, by an even number—which must give us an even number. Hence, in the series of the squares odd and even numbers must follow each other in strict alternation—which, as the second series shows, they actually do. And now, in the third line, I subtracted each square from the next square, which obviously means that, in alternation, I subtracted an odd number from an even number, and then an even number from an odd number. Clearly, when we subtract an even number from an odd number—or an odd number from an even number—the result must again be an odd number. Consequently, the third line, which shows the results of these subtractions, *can* contain only odd numbers. It can also be shown why the subtractions must yield not simply some odd numbers, but all odd numbers in their natural sequence.

Since insight and its temporary absence have now been seen side by side, it will be realized why some European psychologists have always insisted on the essential rôle which insight plays in the solution of problems.

But let us be careful so that we do not exaggerate. Those European psychologists, myself once included, sometimes went a bit too far. Very much impressed by the essential rôle of insight in productive thinking, they often said that the solution of problems is *brought about* by insight—as though nothing else counted. Now this statement is not entirely correct for the following reason. Insight is insight into relations that emerge when certain parts of a situation are inspected. When we consider the situation as first presented to us, insight into certain relations may be a comparatively easy achievement. It may also be easy to recognize that the relations in question give rise to a problem which we have to solve. But what about the solution of this problem? In the solution of a problem, I said, we suddenly become aware of new relations, but these new relations appear only after we have mentally changed, amplified, or restructured the given material. Thus, when we dealt with the diagonal within a certain rectangle constructed in a circle (Figure 25), everything was, of course, clear once we had drawn the second diagonal, which then proved to be identical with the radius of the circle. But why, after inspecting the situation as first given, did we ever think of drawing new lines, and particularly that special line, the second diagonal? Or again, when considering the infinite series $1 - 1/2 + 1/3 - 1/4$, etc., and asking ourselves whether we could say something about the sum of its members, why did it occur to us to group these members as pairs? To be sure, when we did so, certain relations became apparent which gave us the answer, and corresponding insight. But, to repeat, why did we combine the members of the series as pairs within parentheses? After it had happened, we understood, of course, that this was the right procedure. But we could not realize this *until the grouping had been done*. What, then, made us introduce this particular structuring or grouping at a time when we could not yet be aware of its consequences? So it is everywhere, apparently in most cases of productive thinking. No wonder that people who are fortunate enough to solve problems of this kind (or far more important specimens) are invariably surprised by their own achievements. Clearly, the right new relations and corresponding insight emerge only after something else has happened first. Ever since people, mathematicians and others, became interested in the processes that lead to the solution of problems, this aspect of productive thinking has appeared most astounding. Since, for the most part, we do not produce such sudden structurings intentionally, but rather find ourselves suddenly confronted with their emergence, we are forced to conclude that, under the stress of our wish to solve a certain problem—and after our thorough consideration of various parts of the given material— sometimes brain processes tend to assume new forms or structures which, when reflected in our minds, suddenly make us see new relations and thus give us new insights which tend to bring about the solution.

Are there situations in which the rôle of these sudden restructurings in thinking is less conspicuous? What happens when we show a person how a certain problem is solved and then ask him to repeat what, it seems, has just been offered to him ready-made on a platter? When we make actual tests, we find to our surprise that this picturesque expression is sometimes quite misleading. To be sure, subjects often can repeat what they have been shown when the demonstration has been accompanied by explicit verbal statements. Language has many excellent ways of expressing the main relations involved in the solution of a problem. But when the solution consists only of actions which are performed before another person without accompanying remarks, then the task of repeating such actions may become quite difficult, particularly if the essential relations among the parts of the action are many and complicated. I will illustrate the point by describing what happened to a chimpanzee under these circumstances. Some aspects of problem solving are far more clearly seen when the subject is a chimpanzee than when he is a human being. The reason is simply that tasks which we manage to handle without being aware of any difficulties are quite difficult for the ape, especially if the ape is a less intelligent individual.

When trying to solve problems with which they were confronted, the apes I once studied in Africa sometimes made simple inventions. But I also found that, when a particularly intelligent individual had made such an invention, other less intelligent apes were often utterly unable to repeat the action which their brighter companion had just performed before their eyes. Here is an example. Sultan was a clever chimpanzee. He was quite familiar with the solution of the following problem. A banana is attached to the ceiling of the laboratory, far too high to be reached by a chimpanzee even when he jumps. Several yards away from this place, however, is a box of considerable size. In this situation, Sultan never hesitated; he dragged the box until it was just underneath the banana, climbed to its top, and from here jumped up to reach the fruit without the slightest trouble. One would think that when another chimpanzee is present, and sees what is happening, he must afterwards be capable of repeating this simple performance when a new banana is attached to the ceiling and the box is once more given its old position. "Imitation," in this sense, has often been regarded as a particularly easy and natural achievement of monkeys and apes. Now this, I soon had to realize, is a bit of a myth. It does happen that a chimpanzee repeats what others have been doing in his presence—

Figure 26. When the photograph was taken, Rana felt a bit uneasy, and her face exhibits this particular state of mind. She is by no means laughing or smiling—not the first, because chimpanzees never laugh, and not the second, smiling (which they do fairly often), because their smiling looks quite different from the facial expression in the photograph.

always supposing that he is sufficiently interested in that particular action, and that he is sufficiently intelligent to *understand* what he has seen. But a chimpanzee of particularly restricted intellectual gifts may be quite incapable of repeating what another chimpanzee has just done—simply because he has failed to grasp certain relations which are essential to the other's performance. Let me first introduce the subject, whose name was

Rana, which in Spanish, just as in Latin, means "frog." The Spaniards living in the neighborhood had given her this name because her clumsy movements appeared similar to those of a frog. She is shown in Figure 26.

Fortunately, Rana was not only unintelligent, but also particularly eager to go into action, and would thus naïvely demonstrate to an observer just what she failed to understand in a given case. It turned out that Rana simply could not imitate what Sultan had just done with the box. To be sure, she had realized that the box was an important object, for she now jumped up repeatedly from its surface—but without first moving it into the right position. Once she stood on the box in the posture of one who makes ready for a most strenuous action, then quickly jumped to the ground, ran to the place under the banana, and here jumped as high as she could—of course, in vain. The observer's impression was most convincingly that she tried to connect the box and the banana by sheer speed. There was no improvement in several trials so that, eventually, Sultan had to show once more how he did it. Afterwards, it was again Rana's turn. And now she clearly proved that she had entirely failed to understand the most crucial part of Sultan's action. She again approached the box, she also moved it, with great energy in one direction after another, but not in the right one, until at last she gave up and, sitting on the box, looked sadly at the distant banana. Obviously she could not recognize the most essential relation in Sultan's performance— a relation which, in the present case, extends from earlier parts of this performance to later parts. When Sultan begins to move the box, he already moves it *toward the banana.* But, for simple Rana, it is by no means necessary to relate this beginning of the movement to the place where it would later be useful in reducing the gap between the ground and the fruit. To Rana, the beginning of the movement may, for instance, appear as a simple form of playing. Chimpanzees do simply push boxes around when they play. Or she may see the beginning of the movement as a movement away from the original place of the box, which would be a second, but again not the required, relation. Again, the movement might be seen as a movement parallel to one of the walls, and so forth. Why, then, should poor Rana move the box in the *right* direction? Once the box *is* in the right place, she will, of course, realize its value in this place. But this is later in Sultan's performance, and at this later time she is not likely to think back to what happened before and now, retrospectively, grasp the right relation—the relation between the beginning of the movement and the final position of the box under the banana. The right relating of facts across time intervals is an extremely difficult achievement for the Ranas of this world. Mere *seeing* does not guarantee that successive events within a performance are correctly related.

I return now to the rôle of insight in intellectual discoveries which are made without any help from others. Convincing proof that the essential change tends to occur *outside* the mental field, and that only the result appears on the mental stage—such proof is supplied by ever-repeated observations of men who have solved really important problems in science. They all agree on one point. After periods during which one has actively tried to solve a problem, but has not succeeded, the sudden right organization of the situation, and with it the solution, tend to occur at moments of extreme mental passivity. For example, a great chemist found the solution of a fundamental problem in organic chemistry after casually chatting with a friend, while waiting for a streetcar. He just went up the steps of the car, waving to his friend, when suddenly an entirely new possibility of arranging atoms in a molecule appeared before his mental eye. Up to that point, any attempt of his to find the structure of those molecules which would explain their behavior had ended in failure. But now, organic chemistry began to expand in an entirely new direction—after this moment on the steps of the streetcar.

Another experience of this kind occurred to Loewy, then a professor of physiology in Austria. He knew that certain physiologists in England were entertaining a new idea about the way in which nerve impulses, arriving at the heart muscle, accelerate the heart's beat. At the time, it was customary to assume that nerve impulses, being known mainly as electric events, influenced the heart by electric action. But the English scientists had found reason to believe that the nerve impulses are accompanied by minute chemical activities, and that it might be by such chemical action that the impulses accelerate the rhythm of the heart. Professor Loewy, fully aware that the chemical quantities involved had to be minute, and that discovery of such tiny amounts by chemical tests was at the time beyond the power of available techniques, began to think hard about other possibilities where this difficulty would not arise. Nothing worked—he could not solve his problem—until one night when he had just gone to bed. When he had switched off the light, and was already half asleep, abruptly the right answer appeared before him. At this point, I have to add, the story takes an almost tragic turn. Being a cautious man, Professor Loewy thought, "I had better write down the essentials of this marvelous solution." So, in the dark, he took an old envelope and a pencil which happened to be lying on his bedside table and made a few notes on the envelope. The next morning, he immediately remembered that something most fortunate had happened, that now he had the solution to his problem. But precisely what was it? "It does not matter," he thought, "because I remember that I wrote it down on that envelope." He took the envelope and looked at his notes. But there was nothing he could possibly decipher. Being half asleep, and in the dark, he had scribbled something in which no effort of his could discover any sense. Since he could not remember either, he was for a time a most unhappy man—until precisely the same bright idea occurred to him once more, again just before he was falling asleep. This time he not only turned on all lights, but went immediately to his laboratory, in the middle of the night, in order to do the experiment which had occurred to him twice when he was almost asleep. There was no difficulty. The test proved at once, and beyond any possible doubt, that the heartbeat is accelerated by chemical action which accompanies the arrival of certain nerve impulses at the heart. For this achievement Professor Loewy was awarded a Nobel Prize.

I entirely agree with the observation of the great chemist and the great physiologist, that the solution of problems is often suddenly presented to us when we are not actively concerned with them. For my own, far less important, new insights always occur when I am particularly inactive, either when taking a warm bath in the morning or, a bit later, when I am shaving—both situations in which my eagerness to do mental work is exceedingly small. A well-known physicist in Scotland once told me that this kind of thing is generally recognized by the physicists in Britain. "We often talk about the three B's," he said, "the Bus, the Bath, and the Bed. That's where the great discoveries are made in our science."

We have now repeatedly seen that certain outstanding achievements of the mental world do not seem to be achievements of *this* world alone. When we considered the concept of organization in perception, we found that, for the most part, organization as an action does not occur within the mental world. Only the *result* of the organizing process is usually experienced. Now we find that the same holds for certain most important intellectual achievements. These achievements are often made possible by an abrupt reorganization of given materials, a revolution, the result of which suddenly appears ready-made on the mental scene. From where does it come? Where does the revolution as such take place? It can occur only in that strangest of all systems, the brain, which seems, better than the active self, able to do precisely such things—but, to repeat, only when the crucial material has first been thoroughly examined and made ready in active mental work. Why do such revolutions which occur in certain brains tend to be the right revolutions? This is the same question we asked ourselves before: why do brain processes tend to produce perceptual organizations of remarkable clearness of structure? At least this part of nature, the human brain, seems to operate in a most selective fashion. It is the *direction* of its operations which is truly remarkable.

Other Titles of Related Interest
Available in Princeton and
Princeton/Bollingen Paperbacks

AMOR AND PSYCHE: *The Psychic Development of the Feminine*, by Erich Neumann (P/B #239), $2.95

ART AND THE CREATIVE UNCONSCIOUS, by Erich Neumann (P/B #240), $3.45

COMPLEX, ARCHETYPE, SYMBOL IN THE PSYCHOLOGY OF C. G. JUNG, by Jolande Jacobi (P/B #241), $3.45

ESSAYS ON A SCIENCE OF MYTHOLOGY: *The Myth of the Divine Child and the Mysteries of Eleusis*, by C. G. Jung and C. Kerényi (P/B #180), $2.95

FOUR ARCHETYPES: MOTHER/REBIRTH/SPIRIT/TRICKSTER, by C. G. Jung, translated by R.F.C. Hull, Extracted from *The Archetypes and the Collective Unconscious*, Vol. 9, part I, Collected Works (P/B #215), $1.95

FROM CALIGARI TO HITLER: *A Psychological History of the German Film*, by Siegfried Kracauer (#45), $2.95

THE GREAT MOTHER: *An Analysis of the Archetype*, by Erich Neumann, translated by Ralph Manheim (P/B #265), $3.95

JOSEPH CONRAD: *A Psychoanalytic Biography*, by Bernard C. Meyer, M.D. (#188), $2.95

MANDALA SYMBOLISM, by C. G. Jung, translated by R.F.C. Hull, Extracted from *The Archetypes and the Collective Unconscious*, Vol. 9, part I, Collected Works (P/B #266), $3.95

ON THE NATURE OF THE PSYCHE, by C. G. Jung, translated by R.F.C. Hull, Extracted from *The Structure and Dynamics of the Psyche*, Vol. 8, Collected Works (P/B #157), $2.95

THE ORIGINS AND HISTORY OF CONSCIOUSNESS, by Erich Neumann (P/B #204), $3.95

PSYCHOLOGY AND EDUCATION, by C. G. Jung, translated by R.F.C. Hull, Extracted from *The Development of Personality*, Vol. 17, Collected Works (P/B #159), $2.95

THE PSYCHOLOGY OF THE TRANSFERENCE, by C. G. Jung, translated by R.F.C. Hull, Extracted from *The Practice of Psychotherapy*, Vol. 16, Collected Works, (P/B #158), $2.95

THE SOCIAL MEANINGS OF SUICIDE, by Jack D. Douglas (#186), $2.95

SOCIETY AND THE ADOLESCENT SELF-IMAGE, by Morris Rosenberg (#111), $2.95

THE SOCIETY OF CAPTIVES: *A Study of a Maximum Security Prison*, by Gresham M. Sykes (#227), $1.95

THE SPIRIT IN MAN, ART, AND LITERATURE, by C. G. Jung, translated by R.F.C. Hull, Vol. 15, Collected Works (P/B #252), $1.95

THE TASK OF GESTALT PSYCHOLOGY, by Wolfgang Köhler (#267), $2.45

TWO ESSAYS ON ANALYTICAL PSYCHOLOGY, by C. G. Jung, translated by R.F.C. Hull, Vol. 7, Collected Works (P/B #268), $3.95

WHY MEN REBEL, by Ted Robert Gurr (#233), $2.95

Order from your bookstore, or from

Princeton University Press, Princeton, N.J. 08540